MW01100820

CORE PROGRAM COOKING

SECOND EDITION

STEPHEN J. GISLASON M.D.

A guide to food selection, meal-planning, and cooking for the Core Program method of Diet Revision. Recipes in this book are suitable for a range of health needs and can be utilized for:

Food Allergy	**Low Cholesterol**
Weight Reduction	**Low Sugar**
Milk/Dairy-Free	**Low Sodium**
Additive-Free	**Low Salicylate**
Gluten-Free	**Moderate Protein**
High Fiber	**Low Purine**
Low Fat	**High Carbohydrate**
	Additive-Free

VOLUME 4 OF THE NUTRITIONAL MEDICINE SERIES

 PerSona Audiovisual Productions

Copyright © 1989 Stephen J. Gislason & Environmed Research Inc.

First edition 1988
Second edition 1990

Canadian Cataloging in Publication Data

Gislason, Stephen J., 1943 - Core Program Cooking
(Nutritional medicine series/ Stephen J.
Gislason;4)
ISBN 0-9694145-1-X

1. Diet therapy. 2. Food allergy - Diet
Therapy. 3. Nutrition - Popular works.
I. Title. II.Series: Gislason, Stephen J., 1943-
Nutritional medicine series;4.
RM219.G58 1990   641.5'63   C89-091620-9

Nutritional Medicine Series: Core Program

Volume 1. Core Program Nutrition
2. Core Program: Diet Revision Therapy
3. Core Diet for Kids 2nd ed.
4. Core Program Cooking

Cover Photo: Sandra Semchuck
Cover Design: V Group Designs
Printed by Hignell Printing
Typesetting: PerSona Audiovisual Productions
Illustration: Pamela Fajardo, BSc.

Published by:PerSona Audiovisual Productions
#1-3661 West 4th Ave. Vancouver, BC
Canada, V6R 1P2 (604) 731-9168

ACKNOWLEDGEMENTS

This practical volume in the Core Program series owes much of its content to the contributions of patients, co-workers, and friends. Ula Timmermans was the co-author of the first edition of "Core Diet Cooking" and has departed to pursue other goals, but not before contributing in large measure to the re-organization.and contents of this book. The Core program evolved into a 4 phase sequence and Ula worked out the logistics of placing recipes in their proper order and cross-referencing related recipes. I cannot name all the wonderful people who have suggested solutions to the difficult problems of resolving food-related illnesses. Their ability to cope with limited food selection, new menus, unfamiliar methods of meal preparation and planning has been an inspiration to us. Specific recipe suggestions were contributed by the following:

Anna Abel
Janet Bernard
Joyce Cowan
Suzanne Cowan
Beverly Creighton
Dorothy Durstling
Gail Fitzgerald
Pamela Fajardo
Linda Gomez
Catherine Graham
Yvonne Hammond
Donna Haqq
Jan Hughes

Linda Ludford
Marcelle Mason
Josie Nairn
Marlys Robinson
Carol Ann Robinson
Nicole Roy
Randy Rycroft
Linda Saunders
Jennine Stromkins
Hank Suderman
Ruth Weeds
Joanne Weismiller

Thank you all!

Preface

This second, revised edition of Core Program Cooking has been designed to help you succeed with diet revision, and enjoy renewed, healthy eating practices. The Core Program was designed as a practical, therapeutic approach to solving food allergy problems. Everyone has some food allergy and intolerances, mostly undetected. We believe that everyone can benefit from diet revision, using the Core Program method. We have also discovered that the Core Program serves many more diet-revision needs than food allergy alone, and recommend this book, and its companion volumes, to anyone who seeks a healthier approach to eating.

The Core Program is alive and evolving, as we gain experience, helping people recover from a variety of illnesses, using diet revision therapy. The current version has four food-introduction phases. The recipes are now organized to suit the food list at each stage.

The Core Program is first concerned with selecting foods that are compatible with each person's tolerances and needs. We are are all different enough that a "healthy diet" needs to be custom-fitted. Our first priority is good biology, and then we address the culinary issues. Once a food is established as "normal" for your body, you then consider taste, appearance, cost, availability, and nutritional value. In other words: first, you achieve normal body functioning; and second, you seek to please yourself, and your family with meals that look attractive and taste well.

This book was designed to provide more complete food information and to illustrate, with recipe suggestions, the Core Program sequence of meal-planning and preparation. We have attempted to show a progression of recipes, from simple to more complex cooking, following the four phases, described in the companion Core Program books.

The Core Program is a slow food-introduction sequence, which allows us to evaluate how individual foods feel as they interact with our complex digestive, metabolic, and immune-defence procedures. We are so aware of the difficulties of people with food allergy, who lose tolerance to many foods, that we recommend a conservative, thoughtful approach to food selection and meal-planning. We refer to "safe" foods, meaning foods on the Core Program food list that you have screened, for yourself, to rule-out adverse reactions. Once simple basic foods are well-tolerated, we add more foods, slowly increasing the variety and complexity of meal-plans. Single foods, and foods in simple combinations, are easier to evaluate in terms of how you feel after eating them.

Unfortunately, there are no reliable, all-purpose rules of food-combining. Many diet books have suggested food-combining rules that do not work in practice - their authors often argue that certain food combinations do not digest well; but there is no such biological knowledge. Many ethnic groups and religious cultures have food-combining rules which we respect; the Core Program is easily adapted to special food-combining rules. We recommend a high carbohydrate vegetable intake as the basis for a healthy diet, and generally find that fruit and protein foods can be combined with vegetables. This is the style of Asian cooking. Recipes, therefore, are a second level of complexity which you evaluate as you go along. Each person, in our experience, reports individual, and often idiosyncratic, responses to food combinations.

We do suggest that you follow the food-introduction sequence, outlined in the companion volumes "Core Diet for Kids" and "Core Program - Diet Revision Therapy." The Core Program diet-revision strategy is briefly reviewed in the first two chapters of this book. Summaries of the Core Program master food list, and nutritive values for single portions (usually one cup) of Core Program foods are found in the appendix.

We hope this book helps you discover a safe, healthy, and lasting pattern of food selection, cooking, and eating practice.

Stephen J. Gislason M.D.
Vancouver, B.C.
May, 1990

Contents

CONVERSION TABLE

1 tbsp = 3 tsp	1/2 tsp = 2 mL
1/4 cup = 4 tbsp	1 tsp = 5 mL
1/3 cup = 5 1/3 tbsp	1 tbsp = 15 mL
1/2 cup = 8 tbsp	1/4 cup = 60 mL
1 cup = 16 tbsp	1/3 cup = 80 mL
1 fl oz = 2 tbsp	1/2 cup = 125 mL
1 pt = 2 cups	1 cup = 250 mL
1 qt = 2 pts	1 fl oz = 30 mL
1 gal = 4 qts	1 pt = 500 mL
1/8 tsp = 1/2 mL	1 qt = 1 L
1/4 tsp = 1 mL	1 gal = 4 L

Chapter 1

INTRODUCTION TO THE CORE PROGRAM

The Core Program is a sequential diet revision path, designed to re-structure the diets of both children and adults. The Core Program is not a temporary plan, but a long-term healthy eating strategy. We refer to the food selection and meal-plans, emerging from the Core Program as a "Core Diet". Each person develops their own version, a custom-fitted Core Diet. You are encouraged to develop your own menu selections and your own style of cooking. The immediate goals of the Core Diet Program Program are:

1. to alleviate food allergy and other food-related illnesses
2. to assist in resolving abnormal eating behaviors
3. to aid weight control programs
4. to achieve safe superior nutrition.

The design of the Core Diet Program is based on experience solving the problem of food allergies and other food-related illnesses. We now recognize that many people cannot eat all the foods commonly recommended and included in cook books and magazine recipes. The Core Program makes no assumptions about your tolerance for foods. You begin in Phase 1 and eat very simple meals, assembled from basic, healthy foods that you are likely to tolerate well. These foods have a low-allergenic, high- acceptability profile. You proceed by slow, methodical food introductions to diversify your menus, monitoring yourself and other members of your family for recurrent food-related symptoms. The details of Diet Revision techniques are found in the companion Core Program books.

The Core Program includes primary foods, popular all over the world and, at the same time, excludes other foods that are staples in current North American diets, but are often not well-tolerated. Phase 1 can be considered a hypoallergenic diet, designed to remove the most common food allergy problems. This means the complete exclusion of dairy products, eggs, cereal grains, tea, coffee, alcoholic beverages, processed and packaged foods, and other common allergenic foods - peanut butter, nuts, seafoods, citrus fruits, and bananas. It may be that we are rediscovering healthy, staple foods and a basic eating-plan that better suits the ancient design of our digestive tract and metabolism. It may be that we are responding to modern problems of additives and contaminants in our food supply. It may be that our diets have been overloaded with staple but allergenic foods, especially meat, wheat, eggs, and milk.

Whatever the underlying causes of food-related illness, the Core Program is based on successful outcomes in children and adult patients. Core Program food selection is success-oriented, and has no other basis in taste, preference, or ideology. We expect seasonal and regional variation in food quality, and best food choices will vary. Reports from different areas suggest that the Core Program food list is adaptable to people living in most areas of the world.

Dietary recommendations for the prevention and treatment of many diseases tend to converge on several common food choices. The Core Program has been designed to solve several problems simultaneously. Many dietary needs are served by this program. Consult the companion Core Program books for a complete discussion of food-related health problems. The recipes in this book are suitable for adults and children with the following well-promoted, dietary needs:

Food allergy
Weight Reduction
Milk/Dairy-Free
Additive-Free
Gluten-Free
High Vegetable Fiber
Low Fat

Low Cholesterol
Low Sugar
Low Sodium
Low Salicylate
Moderate Protein
High Carbohydrate

1.0.1 The Sequence of Food Introduction

The recipes in this book following the sequence of food introduction presented in the companion Core Program books. Meal planning and preparation proceeds from the simplest meals to more complex varied meals. Phase 1 is the initial clearing food list - the best tolerated, most basic, staple foods. The strategy of diet revision is simple - when the first foods are well-tolerated you advance to the more complex food lists and recipes. When you are not well you retreat to the simpler food-lists and recipes. Each person selects their own best food choices on the Core Diet - not all recipes will be suitable for you. The stages of Core Diet are:

Phase 1 Clearing program: includes staple foods which form the foundation of Core Diet cooking. Not everyone will tolerate all Phase 1 foods - you make your own best selection - alternatives are suggested throughout the cook book.

Phase 2 Initial Food Re-introduction: During Phase 2 you are following a slow, progressive addition of specified foods often with the occasional recurrence of symptoms, and decisions to delete specific foods from the Core Diet list. Your create your own special Safe Food List. Patience, good self-monitoring, and decisions about the acceptability of each food are required. Meals are growing more interesting and more complex.

Phase 3: Stabilization - This stage of the Core Diet is devoted to securing improvements and practicing Core Diet cooking and meal-planning. The new food additions are flavorings and legumes, including soya products. If tofu and soya milk are tolerated many new recipes are available which feature them. The cooking emphasis is on improving appearance of meals, flavors, sauces, and variety.

Phase 4: Expansion of Core Diet - If everything is going well further food introductions are appropriate to further increase the variety of food choices and the palatability of meals. Often, cooking and baking with non-wheat flours is interesting and important at this stage.

Phase 5: Maintenance of an individualized Core Diet has become a successful strategy of healthy self-maintenance over years to come. Meal plans should be complete written-down and followed as a matter of routine. Your own special version of the Core Diet is now normal regular eating practice.

1.0.2 Core Diet Program Food Choices

Our health-seeking goal is to return to a diet of simple, carefully selected, natural foods. Fresh or frozen vegetables, fruit, poultry, and fish are the basic food choices. These are primary foods that allow us to reconstruct daily menus, with confidence of good nutrition, and stable life-long eating habits. Shifting from your old to your new Core Diet cuisine is like moving to a foreign country. You give up your old habits and develop new tastes and preferences. At first you are reluctant. Later you are satisfied with your new habits and may even shun your old cuisine, especially if you react adversely to non-Core Diet foods. The style of Asian cooking, blending different vegetable foods together into a complex and tasty mixture, eaten with rice or millet, is most suitable for Core Diet cooking.

Poultry, fish, and meat options are included in the Core Diet Program but are not essential. A complete vegetarian version of the Core Diet Program is readily achieved by selecting only the rice, vegetable, and fruit options from the core diet and many recipes in this book are suitable. Meat portions are, in any case, much reduced from North American averages. From all points of view, red meat consumption should be minimized, and poultry and fish - carefully selected - are preferred foods.

The Core Diet Program is a natural-food eating plan. Under ideal circumstances, we would all be eating organically grown vegetables and fruits from our own gardens or neighborhood market gardens. For many of us, the garden is a distant retirement dream and we must do our best with store-bought food. Our intention is to simulate eating from the garden by buying and preparing fresh or frozen vegetables, fruit, poultry and fish, according to our own preferences and tolerances.

Core Diet Program foods are simple and common. Most of the desired food is purchased in the regular supermarket or produce store. We would prefer organically grown produce and naturally raised and fed animal foods. Unfortunately, pure uncontaminated food is not always available or is too expensive, and we make due with the food at hand. We occasionally look for unusual rice products, wheat flour substitutes, and dairy substitutes.

The success of the Core Diet Program involves regulating body intake of food with minimal opportunities for biochemical confusion. To simplify the task of food selection, the Core Diet Program plan suggests avoiding foods in bottles, cans, and boxes. If the food has a label on it, we seldom buy it or eat it. There are, of course, exceptions: Core Diet Program recipes may include canned fruit (sugar-free), tuna (packed in water), herbs, and carefully chosen jams, jellies, and sauces. Frozen vegetables, fruit, fish, and poultry are highly recommended - but avoid pre-packaged frozen meals.

Most people learn to use and enjoy more vegetable foods. Vegetable diversity is a key to the success of the Core Diet Program and one of the clearest emerging dietary recommendations from all scientific studies. Increased vegetable intake reduces obesity, coronary artery disease, strokes, cancer, and probably diabetes. Vegetable foods should account for 60-70% of daily calories. Complete if not superior nutrition is possible with vegetable foods alone. Many people are unaware that vegetable foods have enough protein to maintain athletic body-building. The only trick is to combine vegetable foods so that the set of nine essential amino acids is complete. If you mix four vegetables from different botanical families (eg. carrots, peas, broccoli, squash), you tend to get complete amino acid sets. The combination of rice and a legume (peas or beans) is an easy method of completing vegetable protein. It is a Core Diet Program policy to use 3-4 vegetables per meal. If you wish, the addition of small portions of poultry, fish, or red meat easily completes the daily requirement for protein.

1.0.3 Planet Ecology and Food

Our food choices influence the state of planet earth. We suffer the consequences of planet pollution, experiencing illness from contaminated food. We need to respond by seeking better health for ourselves and, at the same time, the planet. Our personal, even selfish interests and the planet Earth's interests turn out to be the same.

We influence economics and politics when we buy food. We can be more selective in food purchases and favor produce, grown without chemical sprays and exposed to the least amount of chemical processing. At the same time we need to be aware that spoilage of food by bacterial and fungal growth is wasteful of agricultural efforts and hazardous to our health. Good food policies balance the need to preserve food values against the hazard of using too many chemicals to avoid spoilage. We need to be more tolerant of surface blemishes on fruit and vegetables, and less than perfect color to avoid the excessive use of chemicals. We should insist on careful food monitoring with daily publication of levels of agricultural chemicals in foods displayed in stores. We need to become better informed consumers, avoiding the personal consequences of chemical contamination, while putting reasonable pressure on farmers and legislators to control the hazards of chemical use. Frozen foods are of high quality and can be made more ecologically sound - food values are well-preserved, spoilage is reduced, and year-round availability is assured. Improved refrigeration technology - more efficient, and without freon will make frozen food options even more attractive. By reducing our intake of meat and other animal products we improve our health, reduce the suffering of animals, and reduce the heavy burden on planet resources that meat production entails.

Francis Lappe made the point in her 1971 book "Diet for a Small Planet" that eating vegetable foods was biologically more efficient than eating animals. A move toward an organic, vegetarian diet saves the planet and spares us at the same time. The Core Program food choices moves us toward a high vegetable market-garden economy, and better quality foods. Other food-morality issues, like the plight of dophins, caught and killed in drag nets by tuna fisherman, can be addressed at the store - a recent announcement by SunKist that they will not market tuna, caught by fisherman who cause dophin deaths, is a welcome change. Obviously, we will support ecologically responsible companies. John Robbins in his startling book "A Diet for New America" [1] makes a strong case of a new level of consumer awareness:

> "We live in a crazy time when people who make food choices that are healthy and compassionate are often considered weird, while people are considered normal whose eating habits promote disease and are dependent on enormous suffering."

---

1. John Robbins A Diet for New America 1987: Stillpoint Publishing; Box 640 Walpole NH 03608

1.0.4 Four Food Groups - Obsolete

We are replacing the "four food groups" method of meal planning with a more appropriate, modern, flexible meal-planning strategy. The four food groups - dairy, grains, vegetables and fruit, and meats - are not suitable or desirable for everyone to eat. Food allergy or other food-related illness change body-input rules and often eliminate one of more of the four food groups.

The exclusion of dairy products, egg whites, and the cereal grains - wheat, rye, oats, and barley - is a firm rule of the Core Diet Program plan in the first 2-3 months at least.

Milk substitutes may include infant soy milk formulas as well as other soy milk and tofu products (including ice cream substitutes).

1.0.5 The Core Diet Program is Gluten-Free

Many Core Diet Program recipes suggest methods of "gluten-free" cookery and baking. Exclusion of wheat, rye, barley, oats is necessary in the initial stages of the Core Diet Program. The exclusion includes all the foods made with the flours of these common grains - Durham flour, triticale, and bulgar are all excluded. The bran of these cereals is also excluded. Our packaged, fast-food, and restaurant food industries rely heavily on wheat flour to produce their products. Gluten-free diets specify food exclusions, including a variety of manufactured foods which contain gluten. Pasta is made with high gluten flour and is off our list of Core Diet Program foods. Gluten exclusion does mean excluding malt, a barley product, and malt-containing beverages - Postum, Ovaltine, beer, and ale. Alcohol is usually excluded, although some tolerance may be found to selected wines and distilled beverages.[*]

Gluten is a name given to the protein fraction of the cereal grains (wheat, rye, oats, barley) which gives them their sticky elastic properties. Gluten elasticity is essential for most breads and baking. Bread is the most desired wheat product and is, unfortunately, the hardest food to duplicate with non-grain flours. The exclusion of cereal grains significantly alters vegetarian regimens, dependent on grains. For most people, rice is the best grain choice. Rice provides the caloric base, the basic "fuel" for the

---

[*]   Campbell JA. Food for celiacs. Journal of the Canadian Dietetic Ass'n. Jan 1982;43(1):20-24.

Core Diet Program. Many Core Diet Program recipes feature rice and alternative baking flours. Rice flour, arrowroot (tapioca), and buckwheat (not a grain) are the most satisfactory wheat flour substitutes. Pasta made with rice flour is readily available in Chinese and Japanese cuisine.

Corn is related to cereal grains and often produces similar allergic reactions. Corn is significantly less tolerated than rice, and is introduced in Phase 4 of the Core Diet Program, in limited amounts. Corn ingestion, in susceptible people, may trigger mood and behavioral changes as well as more explicit symptoms like abdominal gas, pain, or diarrhea. Corn appears in a multitude of products, including snack foods, oils, margarine, and cereals. Corn syrup, and corn starch are the carbohydrate fractions of corn and may be free of allergenic properties. Both can tried as cooking ingredients.

While the exclusion of the four cereal grains makes meal planning and cooking a new and more difficult challenge, there are many substitutes for grain and flour-based foods. Many recipes in this book address the needs of gluten-free baking. These recipes may be unfamiliar and difficult or disappointing at first, but with perserverence tend to produce satisfactory results. Typical bread-dependent "meals" - sandwiches, hamburgers, hot dogs are difficult to simulate on Core Diets and we prefer properly cooked meals in their place.

1.0.6 Rice: Desirable Staple Food

Rice is the staple food chosen for the Core Diet Program because it has low allergenicity, is versatile, is widely available. Rice provides a carbohydrate, caloric base to the diet. Rice comes in many varieties, some of which are sufficiently different to be treated as separate foods. Converted white rice is preferred at the start of the Core Program. Brown rice offers only slightly more nutrients, and some prefer it by taste and texture; however, the husk also contains more potential problems. Rice-eating peoples generally polish their rice, removing the husk. Nutritional arguments, based on the nutrient content of foods outside of the body, may be misleading, if digestion and absorption of nutrients is abnormal. Brown rice and other rice varieties are introduced after tolerance for converted white rice is established. Rice can be utilized in a variety of forms, including rice cereals, rice pablum, puffed rice, rice cakes, rice noodles, rice vermicelli, and rice flour (starch).

Different rices vary sufficiently in taste and texture to maintain culinary interest. Rice may be boiled with sunflower seeds, buckwheat, wild rice, other seeds, and legumes for added variety. All foods, including rice, have the potential to be allergenic, however. The most common symptoms of rice intolerance are fatigue, constipation, bloating and feeling cold.

1.0.7 Grain Alternatives

Buckwheat is an interesting grain-like food to add to your diet, especially if rice is not acceptable because of an adverse response to it. Buckwheat is not a grain, but belongs to the Polygonaceae family which includes sorrel, rhubarb, and dock. Buckwheat is a seed, however, and resembles the grains in having a starchy endosperm; it can be ground into a flour, cooked as a cereal, or prepared as rice. Buckwheat flour is disappointing for baking since it lacks gluten, the elastic, chewy component of bread.

Cassava, an African vegetable, is ground into arrowroot flour; Tapioca is made by heating and moistening arrowroot. Flour is also made from Taro, a Japanese tuber, which is common in Hawaii where poi is a food paste made from Taro roots. Soybeans are versatile and highly nutritious seeds which can be ground and utilized as a flour as well. Other "flours" - amaranth, chickpea and other legume flours - may not be well-tolerated by patients with food allergy and are not featured in Core Diet Program recipes although they remain options in advanced Phase 4 cooking. In studying food-related illness, we are constantly reminded that even the most wholesome food may be harmful to those with allergies, digestive, or metabolic abnormalities.

The 10-15% of people who do not tolerate rice may eat higher caloric vegetables that supply more energy as complex carbohydrate - squash, yams, sweet potatoes, turnips, beets, or carrots are examples.

1.0.8 Social Considerations

Lasting diet change requires self-control, flexibility, and better self-monitoring capabilities. Ideally, we learn to self-monitor and adjust our food choices and eating behaviors as circumstances change. You will be eating more selectively and concentrating on the properties of individual foods for awhile. Allow each food to seem more important than before.

You may be developing a different style of eating from friends and possibly from other members of your family. Different food selection is not always greeted in a friendly and understanding manner. Inform those around you of your decision to proceed with diet revision to seek improved your health and solicit their cooperation.

If you are a wife and mother, cooking for others in your family, call a family conference and explain your intention to develop a new Core Diet Program. Mothers cooking for reluctant children have a specially demanding task which will test your patience and culinary skills. It is unreasonable for the family to expect you to cook two separate meals. It is unreasonable to cook chocolate chip cookies and insist that one family member not eat them. Ask for everyone's cooperation and suggest that the basic food selection on the Core Diet Program will be the basis for family meals. With food allergy, several family members are often afflicted, but perhaps not to the same degree. If the whole family participates in Diet Revision, other family members will often benefit, even when no benefit is anticipated.

If members of your family choose not to follow the program strictly, they can add their own options to the Core Diet Program meals you prepare. It is simpler, of course, if the whole family agrees to join you in your efforts to improve food selection and health.

Married men who do no food preparation must rely on their wife's willingness to alter the menu. Fortunately, most wives are co-operative and are willing to make the necessary effort. It is a good idea to start participating in food selection and preparation, since part of the task of dealing with food intolerances is learning more about the foods you eat, while seeking better control over the foods presented to you.

Single adults often do not prepare and eat proper meals. Eating is a social activity and single people will gravitate to restaurants and cafeterias to satisfy social needs. Often, snacking and fast foods replace properly cooked meals. The Core Diet Program is best followed at home. When you begin, it is essential to cook your own food. Later, carefully selected restaurant meals may be acceptable. Proper food preparation for oneself requires deliberate planning and organization. Replace your snack foods with carrot and celery sticks, or rice cakes with vegetable spreads, jellies or jam.

A change in attitude helps - treat yourself as an honored guest. Avoid eating directly from the fridge or standing at the kitchen counter. Instead, set the table using your best dishes and linen. Serve yourself sparkling water in a wine glass. Prepare a pleasing meal and sit down to enjoy your food. Be efficient - prepare enough food at one meal to have leftovers for the next day. For fast meals, use frozen vegetables, fish, or poultry; these can be quickly thawed and cooked in a steamer or microwave.

1.0.9 Children's Needs

Children respond well to diet change if parents and family are supportive and show approval of new foods. Many mothers struggle with unhappy children and spouses, reluctant to change eating habits, especially if forced to change food selection because of a child's illness. New food choices and cooking techniques are often required and challenge mother's imagination. Remember that young children do not need elaborate recipes, complicated spices, or a lot of sugar to enjoy their food. Simple, regular, repeating meal plans are the ticket to success. You can develop an interesting Core Diet for your children, but avoid being lured by their demands for new foods as entertainment. In our culture food is treated as a reward or a form of entertainment - often with pain and suffering as the result - not pleasure! We see many children with limited food tolerances who would not do well with the more complicated recipes in phase 3 and 4 and recommend concentrating on simpler phase 1 and 2 recipes, at least for the first month of the Core Program. Substitutions for most missing familiar foods can be developed or equally tasty alternatives can be prepared. The recipes in this book should be helpful.

Children should be encouraged to participate in food selection and preparation. Family participation is important to children, who have difficulty if their food is different from everyone else. Develop familiar, "normal" eating patterns at home and try to continue safe eating practices when your child is away from home. Send cooked lunches in food flasks, for example, to school after practising eating this way at home. Remember that children will do as you do, not as you say. Inform the school of your child's eating requirements. If your child visits other homes, send food along and inform the supervising adult of safe foods your child can eat.

Core Diet Program
Path of Diet Revision

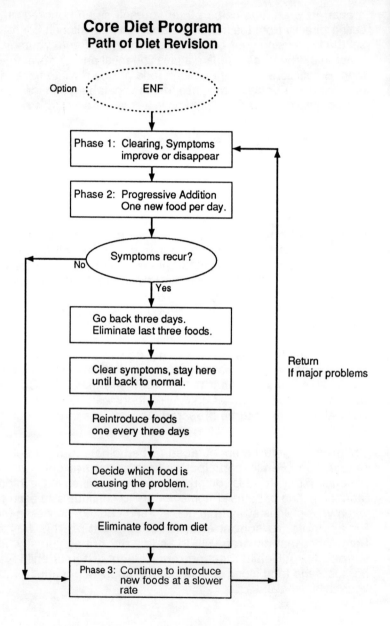

Option ┈ ENF

Phase 1: Clearing, Symptoms improve or disappear

Phase 2: Progressive Addition One new food per day.

Symptoms recur?
No
Yes

Go back three days. Eliminate last three foods.

Clear symptoms, stay here until back to normal.

Reintroduce foods one every three days

Decide which food is causing the problem.

Eliminate food from diet

Phase 3: Continue to introduce new foods at a slower rate

Return
If major problems

Chapter 2

COOKING and MEAL-PLANNING

2.1 Kitchen Practice

Cooking methods can be simple and effective. Part of the strategy of diet revision is to renew the importance of food for the restoration and maintenance of your health and well-being. Complex food mixtures and spicing is not necessary for food to look and taste delicious. A simple appreciation of basic foods can increase our pleasure in cooking and eating. Edward Brown, in the introduction to his excellent book "Tassajara Cooking",[**] suggests:

> *"Cooking is not a mystery*
> *The more heart we put out*
> *the more heart we put in.*
> *To bring cooking alive*
> *we give our life. Giving*
> *our life willingly we don't*
> *get put out.*
> *Washing cutting cooking cleaning,*
> *exploring ways to give life to our life..."*

When you have the time and inclination, food preparation takes on spiritual and poetic significance. The slicing of a carrot or cabbage is kitchen art, as you pause to admire the design and color of nature's gifts. We may lack the time and energy to prepare pleasant meals and deprive ourselves of the luxury of patient, appreciative food preparation.

[**]   Brown EE. Tassajara cooking. Boulder, Colorado: Shambala Publ. Inc., 1973.

Often we need quick, functional solutions to meal construction. We want convenience, quick pleasures, and, most of all, little or no interruption of habitual patterns. But real solutions to real problems do require interruptions, inconveniences, and changes in habits which are as difficult as they are effective. Edward Brown suggests:

> *"You follow recipes, you listen to advice, you go your own way. Even wholehearted effort sometimes falls short, the best intentions do not insure success. There is no help for it, so go ahead, begin and continue: with yourself, with others, with vegetables...The way to be a cook is to cook..."*

2.1.1 Efficiency in the Kitchen

In a practical sense, your kitchen becomes your personal chemistry laboratory where your recipes for better health are carefully put together and records of your progress are kept. You start to think of the 40 or so nutrients that our bodies need to extract from the food you prepare and eat. You want to minimize exposure to any substances that are not nutrients. You want to balance nutrient intake so that each person's metabolism functions like a finely-tuned engine. You will need to identify and remove problem-causing substances.

You may have to reorganize your kitchen. After you have discarded, given away, or put away foods which are excluded in the Core Program, make a shopping list for Core Diet foods and stock up on them. Create a spot for your records - a wall board for posting food-lists and reminders is helpful. You will need to keep a daily food-symptom journal; this is your laboratory notebook, essential to your personal investigation of your food tolerances.

Spend more time in the kitchen in order to have better control of your food supply. Planning ahead can increase your efficiency. Cook enough for a few meals at one time. Leftovers should not be frowned upon as they reduce time in the kitchen! In fact, soups and stews often taste better the longer they are simmered. Leftovers from supper, for example, can be used for the following day's breakfast or lunch.

Make large amounts of foods at one time and divide them into meal-sized portions. Freeze these so you have meals handy (use tinfoil or tin/plastic plates to freeze several foods together to make "TV Dinners"). Reheat foil-wrapped dinners in the oven or plastic-wrapped dinners in the microwave. Frozen vegetables are a great boon to a busy schedule - buy frozen mixed vegetables (eg. peas and carrots) to have a vegetable variety readily available.

Microwave ovens are a good choice for efficient meal preparation. They are energy efficient and ecologically sound. They are also useful for reheating leftovers, or thawing frozen foods.

2.1.2 Cooking Techniques

Cooking has several important functions; there are many heat labile and potentially troublesome substances in vegetables and fruit foods which we want to alter by adequate cooking. Cooking denatures some protein and otherwise reduces antigenic molecules. Cooking also softens food and liberates enzymes from ruptured plant cells, promoting easier digestion. All vegetables contain undigestable carbohydrate fiber as well as other indigestible molecules, some of which are toxic prior to cooking.

Chewing food well is the initial step toward digestion and is rather important, especially if you are having bowel symptoms. Purees aid digestion and are achieved by putting lightly steam-cooked vegetables or fruits into a blender or food processor and adding water as necessary to blend the mixture; soups, juices, and thick purees for use as spreads are easily made this way.

Uncooked vegetables, while nutritionally and esthetically very desirable, are less easily digested. Cook all vegetables initially, preferably by steaming. They should be either fresh or frozen not canned, nor packaged if you can avoid it.

Well-cooked vegetables may lose a small fraction of their nutritive value, but are easier to digest, and contain fewer problematic molecules - important advantages, especially in the early stages of the Core Diet. Many people find that extra cooking significantly reduces digestive problems and food allergic responses. The people who passionately advocate eating only raw fruit and vegetables do not seem to have practical experience in helping people recover from food allergy and other food-related illness.

Treat the food you are preparing as you would a special friend. Use clean utensils for preparing and eating food. Rinse all your dishes, pots, and utensils very well to rid them of detergent. Wash all fruits and vegetables and peel them whenever possible.

Steaming is the preferred method of cooking vegetables; steam them using a stainless steel or bamboo basket in a covered pot. Most vegetables and fish steam in under 10 minutes. Steamed foods retain their vitamins and minerals, as well as their flavors and colors. Steaming several different foods or small dishes at once is an oriental style of eating. The Chinese call it "dim sum" when small portions of varieties of succulent steamed foods are served for meals between breakfast and late afternoon.

Poaching tenderizes foods and keeps them moist. Place the food in a pan on the stove and immerse the food in a liquid with no added fat (water, safe juice, or defatted stock, for example). Cover the pan and simmer the liquid gently (never boil the liquid rapidly). Add herbs to the liquid for flavoring, if desired. When the food is poached, reserve the liquid for a soup or a sauce. To create a sauce, remove the poached food and reduce the poaching liquid (ie. over medium-high heat, evaporate some of the liquid to concentrate the flavor), then stir in a pureed vegetable.

Pressure Cookers are airtight and cook using superheated steam. They reduce cooking time by as much as two-thirds. Some vegetable and fruit problems are removed by pressure cooking - people with little food tolerance may find this cooking method very helpful. Hold temperatures above 100 degrees Celsius (212 F) for 10-15 minutes to achieve the denaturing effect.

Microwave Cooking appears to be safe and effective - try to achieve the same vegetable consistency that steaming achieves. Microwaved vegetables retain maximum nutrients, flavor, and color. Moist products are achieved without added fat. The microwave is also useful for defrosting frozen foods or reheating leftovers.

Rice Cookers are convenient applicances - wash rice until the water runs clear and add the required amounts of water, push the cook button and in 20-30 minutes you have perfectly cooked rice. Read directions on rice packages to find the proper ratios for rice and water. Usually a 1 cup of rice and 1 1/4 cup water is the usual. It is also convenient for use with cook-ins and hot pot recipes. When getting up in the morning and breakfast calls for cooked rice, you can have the rice cooking unattended while you get ready for your day. Most rice cookers also keep the cooked rice warm until ready to eat.

Sauteing is a quick cooking method which browns foods. Use a large, shallow-sided pan over medium to high heat. Use a small amount of oil and heat it (but do not let it smoke). Make sure the pan is large enough for liquid to evaporate, otherwise you will be steaming the food rather than sauteing it. Fibrous vegetables or large pieces of food should be parboiled before sauteing to tenderize them and reduce sauteing time. If the foods brown too quickly, carefully add a tablespoon or two of water and continue cooking until the water evaporates. Stir the foods or shake the pan frequently to prevent the food from sticking. Non-stick sauteing minimizes oil use while sauteing; use a non-stick pan (fish, for example, will saute in a few drops of oil).

Wok Cooking can be used to saute then steam food in attractive, tasty combinations. Routine Core Diet meals are best prepared in a wok. "Stir-frying" is acceptable; however, it is best to only use high temperature sauteing for the first 2-3 minutes; then turn the heat down.

Introduce sliced or cubed poultry, fish, meat, or tofu first and sautee. Then introduce vegetables and/or cooked rice sequentially, beginning with the vegetables requiring the most cooking. Stir-fry vegetables briefly, then add water to the wok and cover it with a lid to finish the cooking by steaming.

Use safflower, olive, or canola oil to stir-fry (2-3 teaspoons per meal or less if you want minimal fat intake). A touch of sesame oil may be added for flavor. It is not desirable to use large amounts of vegetable oil. Never allow the oil to get hot enough to bubble, splatter, or smoke; overheated vegetable oils oxidize rapidly into toxic compounds. Do not use animal fat nor melted margarine for cooking.

Chinese-style cooking: Use a wok or skillet to heat oil (do not use high heat as you do not want the oil to smoke). First add any poultry, fish, or meat, chopped into bite-sized pieces. Saute 2-4 mins, then add vegetables, chopped into bite-sized pieces, and any safe herbs or spices. Saute another 2-4 mins. Add 1/4-1/2 cup water and cover, steaming for 2-4 mins over medium heat. Remove the lid and make a well in the center of the vegetables. Dissolve 1 tsp Tapioca starch (if tolerated) in 1/3 cup water and pour this into the well. Increase the heat to cook the Tapioca starch, stirring to coat the vegetables. The Tapioca starch solution serves as a sauce and seals in the vegetables' flavors and nutrients.

Flavoring of foods can be achieved by using salt, pepper, herbs, and/or spices. Use modest amounts of salt when cooking rice and vegetables. Sea salt has the advantage of extra minerals. Often, we want increased potassium intake; potassium chloride is sold as an alternative salt to regular table salt (sodium chloride). Product names include "Nu Salt" and "No Salt". Flavoring is best achieved with simple culinary herbs. Initially, we avoid hot spices including ginger, garlic, onion, cinnamon, cloves, chili, paprika, and curry, since these are potent spices with druglike effects, and many patients have problems with them. Eventually you may try them again, but, in the beginning, it is advisable to keep your food simple.

2.1.3 Core Program Phases

The Core Program involves a sequence of food introductions in 4 phases. Phase 1 recipes are simple, basic recipes, which evolve, by adding or replacing ingredients with foods introduced in later stages of the Core Program. If your food tolerance permits, additional foods and cooking ideas allow increasingly varied and interesting menus. For example, a basic cooked vegetable salad consists of cooked carrots, green beans, and peas tossed in an oil and water dressing. You could modify this basic recipe in Phase 1 by adding or substituting cubed cooked zucchini, diced canned peaches, shredded cooked poultry, or chopped parsley to the salad, and salt to the dressing. In Phase 2, you could use boiled diced turnip instead of the beans, diced avocado instead of the peaches, and cubed cooked beef instead of the poultry, and add sugar to the dressing. In Phase 3, you could modify the basic recipe using foods from all three Phases. You could add cooked chickpeas, substitute the fruit with sunflower seeds and the beef with cubed tofu, add minced dill weed, or use an oil and vinegar dressing. Modifying the salad in Phase 4 might mean using sauteed mushrooms, raisins, or shrimp in the salad, or garlic powder in the dressing. The options are yours to discover!

Some recipes are designated *P1 - P4*; this means a modified version of this recipe appears in a later Phase (or Phases) of the Core Diet Program.

2.2 Meal Planning

As food choices increase and meal plans grow more complex, it helps to work out standard meal-plans for the week. The Core Program strategy is to vary your choice of "safe" foods so that you are not eating the same foods every day. The variety and mix of the different foods assures you will receive a spectrum of nutrients and also minimizes the negative effects of minor adverse reactions to single foods.

As you advance through the Core Program, you may discover further adverse reactions to food, especially with increased complexity of food combinations. The ingredient list of a recipe may be altered to avoid symptoms from single ingredients. Treat the recipe as a sketch of a desirable meal, and improvise with your own variations on the ingredient list. It is a good idea to keeps notes as you try recipes so that you will remember successes and failures.

An adequate diet plan consists of 3 to 4 balanced meals per day. The actual amount of food eaten should be determined by your appetite, which, we hope, will work in a more balanced and physiological manner, adjusting your food intake to your needs. It is important to eat properly-prepared, well-balanced meals early in your activity day.

2.2.1 2/3's Rules

Since we are replacing meal-planning by the "four food groups", we need simple guidelines for distributing our foods during the day. **Three simple 2/3 rules help us select and distribute foods on the Core Diet:**

1. Vegetable foods (including rice, rice products, or other grain alternatives) should account for two thirds (2/3) of your daily calories. The other 1/3 of daily calories is supplied as fruit, fish, poultry or meat and fat as vegetable oil.

2. Cook approximately 2/3 of your vegetable foods and eat the rest as fresh, raw salad or snack vegetables. If you have digestive difficulties or other symptoms with raw vegetables, simply cook all the vegetables.

3.   About 2/3 of your daily calories should be eaten by late afternoon (or within 8 hours of waking). For most people, this means increasing the amount of food eaten at breakfast and especially at lunch. We recommend fully-cooked, complete lunch meals.

A more specific food proportioning plan is desirable as you advance toward fully defining your own long-term Core Diet. If we define a portion as 1 cup of cooked food or equivalent, a first approximation of a daily food allowance would be:

Distribute your available foods in approximately the proportions listed below:

FOOD GROUPS	PORTIONS
Rice, Rice Products	2-3/day
Vegetables Cooked	4-6/day
Vegetables Uncooked	3-4/day
Fruit	2/day
Meat, Poultry, Fish, Tofu	1-2/day
Vegetable Oil	1-3 tsp/day
Water	1.0 liter/day

For most people these proportions would require a dramatic increase in the intake of vegetable foods - a good idea from all points of view! Rice portions may be replaced by other grain alternatives, or by higher caloric vegetables, if rice allergy is a problem. On a strict vegetarian Core Diet, the poultry-fish-meat option can be replaced by tofu, other soya products, and/or other legumes (if tolerated). If protein intake is restricted by severe food allergy, free amino acids can be supplied as an elementary nutrient formula (ENFood) to supplement vegetable sources of protein.

Chapter 3

PHASE 1   CLEARING DIET

There are twelve common staple foods available during the clearing phase of the Core Program which should last at least ten days. These foods are identified as "Phase 1 Foods" and are important for long-term eating success. Our first goal is to eliminate all problematic foods and to determine which foods are safe to eat.

Phase 1 recipes are simple ways of presenting the best-tolerated, basic foods in their close-to-natural state. These recipes will not compete with recipes in gourmet cookbooks, but will guide you towards a new healthy way of cooking. Some people feel so much better on Phase 1 foods that they prefer to eat them on a regular basis and return to them whenever they deviate from the Core Diet Program and feel ill. Phase 1 foods are our best choices, a refuge in the otherwise confusing world of prolific food choices.

Since food choices are limited during the intial clearing phase of the Core Diet, no distinction is made between breakfast, lunch, and dinner. The food program resembles infant feeding. You cook and eat the same healthy foods 3 or 4 times per day. The major change is to eat increased amounts of cooked vegetables - for breakfast, lunch and dinner! Do not be discouraged by the "limited" selection; instead, view this experience as a healing or cleansing exercise. Over time you may often return to phase 1 foods for rest and recuperation. We encourage developing and intimate, trusting relationship with these staple safe foods!
Water is the principle beverage of the Core Diet. It can be served hot or cold. Bottled water - distilled or carbonated may be desirable; check local suppliers for quality assurances.

Phase 1 Food List

Vegetables

Broccoli
Carrots
Green Beans
Peas
Squash
Yams
Zucchini

Rice Products

Converted Rice
Rice Cakes

Rice Cereal

Fruit

Peaches
Pears

Poultry Option

Chicken
Turkey

Vegetable oils

Olive Oil

Safflower Oil
Sunflower Oil

Flavorings

Basil
Oregano
Parsley
Pepper
Rosemary
Salt
Thyme

Water

Vegetarian Substitution: If you prefer to avoid poultry (and other meat options) you can substitute another vegetable for the poultry option - combining rice with peas or green beans for each meal to improve the intake of essential amino acids; also add 1-2 teaspoons of vegetable oil. You may also add a small amount (1-2 ounces per day) of tofu to increase protein intake. Tofu is soya protein and is not always well-tolerated. Double-check your tofu tolerance if you choose this option.

Often we organize Phase 1 foods into 4 groups, in order of priority of introduction. Establish Group A food first and then proceed through Group B and so on.

Group A: Rice, chicken, carrots, peaches
Group B: Peas, yams, squash, pears
Group C: Green beans, turkey, broccoli, zucchini
Group D: Salt, oil, pepper, flavoring herbs

Cooked vegetables are the most important part of the Core Diet. Cooking vegetables makes them easier to digest and are generally better-tolerated than raw vegetables. Vegetables can be prepared a number of different ways. Carrots, for example, may be boiled, steamed, stir-fried, microwaved, or sauteed. Cooked carrots may then be eaten as is, seasoned with herbs such as parsley or basil, mashed, pureed into soup, added to rice, mixed with other vegetables, used as stuffing, or juiced.

3.0.1 Profiles of Phase 1 Foods

Broccoli (Brassica oleracea, variety italica) developed from wild cabbage. It has a high water content (over 90%) and is low in calories with fewer than 50 Kcal per 1 cup cooked broccoli - 1 cup of cooked broccoli provides about the same amount of protein (5g) as 1 cup cooked corn or rice, but less than 1/3 the calories (95 Kcal vs 150-299 Kcal in cooked cereals). It contains approximately equal amounts of calcium and phosphorus and is a fair to good source of iron, an excellent source of potassium, Vitamin A, and Vitamin C, and a good source of bioflavonoids. Broccoli with thick, woody stems and buds which are beginning to flower is too old, even though it may be green. Choose broccoli with tender yound buds which are tiny and tightly packed. Cook broccoli well to denature gas-producing substances. Frozen broccoli is available, but fresh is far superior in taste and texture.

Carrots are members of the parsley family (Umbelliferae), related to caraway, celery, dill, fennel, parsley, and parsnips. They are the richest source of Vitamin A among the commonly used vegetables - a 100g serving provides more than double the RDA of Vitamin A for adults. Carrots are high in water (88-92%) and low in calories (29-42 Kcal per 100g). Cooked carrots furnish only 2/3 of the calories supplied by raw carrots and carrot juice, but have a higher water content. Small, young carrots have a better flavor than older carrots, which may have a woody core. Soak large carrots in water before preparing them to add crispness. Wash and peel carrots before use. Frozen carrots may be purchased alone or mixed with other vegetables such as peas.

Snap (Green) Beans belong to the Family Leguminosae, Phaseolus vulgaris. Immature beans are called snap, string, or green beans. "Snap" beans can refer to many varieties of both green and wax (yellow pod) beans. Snap beans are more than 90% water and have more calcium than phosphorus. They also provide ample amounts of iron and potassium per calorie and are a better source of Vitamins A and C than are dried beans. Choose the smallest, crispest beans - they should "snap" when broken. Cook beans in rapidly boiling water for a crisp, fresh flavor without the raw edge. Frozen beans are handy when you are in a hurry.

Garden Peas (Pisum sativum), when cooked, provide half the solids, calories, carbohydrates, and proteins of cooked dried peas. They are a good to excellent source of Vitamin A and a good source of Vitamin C. Peas are much lower in calcium and phosphorus than beans. They are a good source of iron and potassium. 1 cup cooked green peas provides 8g protein, equivalent to that in 28g of cooked lean meat, but at twice as many calories per gram of protein. They provide 7.5g protein per 100 Kcal (almost as much protein as eggs). Pea protein is deficient in methionine and cystine. Do not overcook frozen peas or they will become mushy. If you are using frozen peas in a recipe, try to add them at the last moment so they retain their shape.

Squash fruits (flesh and seeds) and flowers are edible. On the Core Diet, we opt to eat the fruits only. Squash is a member of the gourd or melon family (Cucurbitaceae) which also includes pumpkins and cucumbers. Certain varieties of fruits within these species are pumpkins rather than squash. Summer squash are immature, and have a soft, watery flesh. They contain more than 95% water and are very low in calories (14 Kcal/100g) and most other nutrients. They are a fair source of potassium and Vitamin A and C (the yellow and dark green varieties generally are richer in Vitamin A than the white and pale green ones). Summer squash include white or creamy-white (eg. White Bush Scallop), yellow (straight or crookneck), and green, green-black, or green-stripped varieties. Summer squash is best steamed, but zucchini may be sauteed, stuffed and baked, or French-fried. Winter squash are mature, hard-skinned, and have a mildly-flavored, finely-grained flesh. Baked winter squash has a lower water content (85%)

than most other cooked vegetables. It has more than 4 times the calories, twice the potassium, and 10 times the Vitamin A of summer squash and is an excellent source of Vitamin A (the yellow-orange flesh varieties contain the most). Varieties include green (eg. Acorn), buff (eg. Butternut), green or golden (eg. Delicious), and those containing spaghetti-like pulp (eg. Spaghetti). Winter squash can be baked or steamed.

Yams belong to the Family Dioscoreaceae, genus Discorea. They are not related to the sweet potato, although some varieties of the latter are sometimes mislabelled as yams. Sweet potatoes may be substituted for yams in Phase 1 as they are both generally well-tolerated and can be cooked in a similar manner. Compared to potatoes, yams contain about 50% more calories, about the same amount of protein, and half the Vitamin C. Yams are a fair to good source of calcium, phosphorus, and iron. They contain almost no carotene.

Sweet potatoes, in comparision to potatoes, contain the same amount of calories, less protein and Vitamin C, and more Vitamin A (they are a very good source of this vitamin). 1 cup of cooked sweet potato provides 275 Kcal and 5g protein, about twice as many calories and as much protein as found in 1 cup of cooked rice or corn. Yams have white or yellow flesh and a potato-like texture, while sweet potatoes may be sweet, soft, and have yellow to orangey-red flesh (these are often mistaken for yams) or may be dry, mealy, and have pale yellow flesh. Yams, like potatoes, can be fried, boiled, mashed, or baked. Sweet potatoes are more versatile; they can be sauteed, fried, baked, boiled, mashed or pureed, added to casseroles, or used in baking or as pie filling.

3.0.2 Rice

Rice is an annual grass of the Gramineae family (Oryza sativa). There are several thousand cultivars of rices; long-grain rice has a high amylose content relative to medium and short-grain rice. We begin the Core Diet with Uncle Ben's converted white rice; converted or parboiled rice steams well. Parboiled rice is parboiled before the milling process to remove surface starch. Rice without hulls is 80% starch, 8% protein, and 12% water. The nutrient content of rice is similar to wheat and better than corn. Cooked rice is either dry or soft; dry is the usual main food of a meal while soft is more like a gruel and is achieved by cooking small amounts of rice in large amounts of water. Soft rice is usually used for breakfasts or desserts. There are a multitude of ways to cook dry rice; regardless of the method, the ultimate goal is to produce thoroughly cooked rice with separate grains. Even when cooking softer rice, all the moisture should be absorbed by the grains.

Rice becomes your staple food, if tolerated. It can be boiled or steamed a number of ways, in water or in flavored liquids. Experiment to find a method that satisfies you. Rice can also be baked; fried; seasoned; mixed with fruit, vegetables, or poultry; used in a salad, stuffing, or sauce; added to soups or stews; or used for puddings or frozen desserts. Rice cakes (made from puffed rice) become bread and cracker substitutes in this Phase. Puffed rice cereal is a breakfast option. Puffed rice can also be used as a coating for poultry. Rice noodles made from rice and water may be tried towards the end of Phase 1. These may be served like wheat pasta or added to soups.

3.0.3 Fruit

Fruit choices are limited in Phase 1. Peaches and pears are first introduced, and may be canned (in a preservative-free sugar-free syrup) Cooked (preserved and canned) fruits tend to be better tolerated than fresh, raw fruit. Peaches are classified as drupes, genus Prunus, and are closely related to apricots, almonds, cherries, and plums. They are essentially the same as nectarines which lack the fuzz of peaches (both are Prunus persica). Pears are pomes, closely related to the apple and quince. North American pears are either the Oriental sand pear, the common European variety, or a cross between the two. Canned peaches and pears and their juice are quite versatile. The juice can be used instead of milk to moisten cereal and it can be browned to make gravy. The fruit can be added to cereal, rice, salads, stuffing, beverages, and frozen desserts.

3.0.4 Poultry

ChickenIXMASTER Chicken and Turkey are introduced in Phase 1. The white meat (eg. breast) tends to be associated with fewer problems than the dark meat (eg. thighs, drumsticks). The least problematic form of poultry meat is deboned, skinned, defatted breast meat. Problems have been associated with cooking chicken bones and soup bases (and commercial soup products) from boiled carcasses are avoided whenever possible. Both chicken and turkey are higher in quality protein and lower in fat than beef and pork. They are a rich source of all the essential amino acids, a good source of phosphorus, iron, copper, and zinc, and a rich source of Vitamins B-12 and B-6. Poultry supplies appreciable amounts of Vitamin A, biotin, niacin, pantothenic acid, riboflavin, and thiamin. Chicken and turkey can be roasted, barbecued, poached, boiled, steamed, sauteed, stir-fried, microwaved, or pressure-cooked. Poultry is suitable in soups and stocks, stews, and salads; added to rice or vegetable dishes; or served with stuffing or seasoned. Avoid "self-basting" turkeys as they are injected with butter, oil, or fat to lubricate and moisten the meat during roasting. Keep size in mind when purchasing a whole bird; an 8 lb (about 3.5 Kg) turkey will serve four with plenty of leftovers.

The poultry options can be omitted to create a vegetarian version of the Core Diet.

3.0.5 Oils

Vegetable oils are used for cooking and for salad dressings. In Phase 1, a basic oil and water dressing can be used as a sauce for cooked vegetables or to toss cooked vegetable, rice, or rice noodle salads. We discourage the use of large amounts of any fat. Oils derived from plant matter are preferred over fats of animal origin. Olive Oil is one of the most easy to digest oils. Its fatty acid content is 75% oleic, 13% palmitic, 9% linoleic, 2% stearic, and 1% palmitoleic. It is a monounsaturated fat and seems to reduce LDL ("bad" cholesterol) while keeping HDL ("good" cholesterol) levels stable. Safflower Oil, derived from a relative of the thistle, is an excellent source of the essential fatty acid, linoleic acid (77%) and contains 16.4% oleic acid. Sunflower Oil is another excellent sources of linoleic acid, at 66%, with oleic 21%, palmitic 8%, and stearic 5%. Both safflower and sunflower oils are polyunsaturated fat and may contribute to lower LDL and HDL cholesterol levels. Linseed Oil and sesame oil may be used in Phase 1 as an options .

3.0.6 Flavorings

Flavor additions can make a big difference in a recipe. Although this Phase stresses the preparation of simple meals, by adding seasonings of your choice you can enliven a prospectively "bland" meal. The herbs Parsley, Oregano, Rosemary, Thyme and Basil add light flavors to soups, stews, rice and vegetable dishes, poultry, stuffings and salad dressings while pepper adds a sharper flavor. Salt (sodium chloride) can be used in cooking water to bring out the natural flavor of vegetables. Use salt in moderation.

3.1 Rice Cooking

Rice is the first desirable staple food tried; 2-4 cups of cooked rice per day provides a caloric base for your diet. We begin with Uncle Ben's converted white rice, and once tolerance to this well-tolerated rice is established we try other types of rice in Phase 2 and 3.

Rice cakes and puffed rice cereal may be introduced in Phase 1 as supplements to cooked rice. Keep in mind, however, that 1 cup of puffed rice/rice cakes is equivalent to approximately 1/2 cup cooked rice so you have to eat twice as much puffed rice to get the same number of calories as from cooked.

Rice cakes are important as substitutes for wheat-based bread and crackers. Start with plain rice cakes (salted if you prefer). Rice cakes made from brown rice have been well-tolerated although brown rice itself is not appropriate at this stage. Introduce rice cakes with sesame seeds, buckwheat, and millet later. Rice-based crackers can also be introduced in the later stages of the Core Diet.

Puffed rice or cooked rice cereal (try Heinz Infant Rice Cereal) is a breakfast option. Rice-based commercial cereals, such as Rice Chex, Rice Flakes, and Rice Krispies, are available, but are associated with some tolerance problems; reserve these for later introduction and evaluate them carefully.

Rice noodles or vermicelli are available; those made from rice and water may be introduced in Phase 1.

Steamed Rice #1
1 cup Uncle Ben's converted white rice
2-3 cups water

Wash the rice repeatedly, discarding the water. Add 2-3 cups of water; boil for 3 mins and discard the water. Put the rice in a rice steamer and steam for 30 mins to 1 hour.

Steamed Rice #2
1 cup Uncle Ben's converted white rice
2-3 cups water

Wash the rice and discard the water. Add 2-3 cups of water; boil for 5 mins and discard the water. Place the rice into individual bowls, filling 3/4 full to allow room for expansion. Steam over medium heat for 1-1 1/2 hours. Check occasionally to ensure there is enough water for steaming, but not so much that it floods the bowls; add water as necessary.

Boiled Rice
1 cup Uncle Ben's converted white rice
2 cups water

Wash the rice and discard the water. Add 2-3 cups of water. Heat to boiling over high heat, then use low heat. Cover and cook about 20 mins or until steam is visible around the edge of the lid (do not remove the lid too soon or the cooking process will be interrupted). When properly cooked, the rice will be soft and dry, not hard and wet. This recipe can be increased; simply maintain the proportions of 2 cups water per 1 cup rice. For very soft rice, use an extra 1/2 cup water per cup of rice.

Indonesian Rice
Choose a saucepan appropriate for the amount of rice you are cooking. Wash the rice repeatedly and remove any discolored grains. Shake the pan so all the rice is on the bottom of the pan in an even layer. Put your index finger on the rice so it just touches the surface and add sufficient water to reach the first knuckle on your finger. Remove your finger and put the saucepan on the stove on maximum heat. When the water boils, cover and reduce heat to low (you might want to place a wire cooking star on the element at this point to prevent the rice from sticking to the pan, although this is not necessary with sufficient water). Simmer 20 mins (do not open the lid before the time is up). Uncover and fluff the rice. If it seems too damp, too much water was added, so leave the pan uncovered on the heat for a few more minutes, watching it carefully. If the rice appears uncooked, too little water was added, so add a bit more and leave the pan uncovered on the heat a little longer.

Flavored Rice
Use chicken/turkey stock instead of the required water or safe juice for half of the required water. You can also add chunks of canned peaches/pears, grated carrot, or peas to the rice prior to cooking.

Leftover Rice
Add leftover cooked rice to soups and stews, or make deep-fried rice cakes.

Reheating Cooked Rice #1: Heat water in the bottom of a double boiler. Heat the cooked rice in the top until it is hot and fluffy (about 10 mins).

Reheating Cooked Rice #2: Use a pan with a tightly fitting lid. Put the rice in the pan and sprinkle it with water (about 2 tbsp per cup of rice). Cover and cook over low heat until the rice is hot and fluffy (about 5-8 mins). Be sure the heat is not too high or the rice may burn on the bottom.

Refrigerating Cooked Rice: Place the cooled rice in a bowl and cover it tightly to prevent it from drying out. Refrigerated rice will keep 4-5 days. Rice that has gone bad will have a overly sweet smell. To use refrigerated rice, follow the directions for reheating cooked rice.

Freezing Cooked Rice: Put the cold rice in a covered freezer container or wrap it well. Frozen rice will keep up to 6 months. To use it, thaw it and follow the directions for reheating cooked rice.

Green Rice: Mix finely chopped parsley with cooked Uncle Ben's converted white rice and season with salt.

Rice Casserole: Stir together cooked Uncle Ben's converted white rice, a chopped or grated carrot, and a spoonful or two of turkey stock. (Cubes of cooked turkey or canned peaches/pears may also be added to taste). Heat in the oven in a casserole dish.

Rice in Foil: Place cooked Uncle Ben's converted white rice and grated raw carrot on a piece of foil. Fold up edges to make a pouch; before sealing, add 1-2 tsp water or fruit juice. Heat in the oven or on the barbecue.

Deep-fried Rice Cakes: Use 200g cooked rice and 4 dL safe oil.
Preheat the oven to 190C. On a non-stick cookie sheet, place mounds of rice (4 tbsp per mound) and flatten them. Bake the cakes for 35 mins, until they are yellow-brown. Heat the oil on high in a wok. Put the cakes in the oil and deep-fry them until they are golden brown. These cakes will keep a couple of days.

Molded Rice: Cook 4 cups of Uncle Ben's converted white rice. Oil a 4-cup Jello mold or Bundt cake pan and press the rice lightly into it. Keep hot until served. To serve, invert a plate on the mold and turn the mold over. Remove the mold.

Fried Rice and Variations: Stir fry ingredients such as chicken, peas, and chopped vegetables adding 1 tsp of water then adding rice. Season with safe herbs. Make this in large quantities and keep in the fridge for snacks, breakfasts and side dishes.

Variations: Turkey, peach cubes, chopped zucchini, thinly sliced green beans. Stir fry dishes with a saucy juice (water) can be served on a bed of fried rice or plain rice.

3.2 Vegetable Dishes

Vegetables are a major component of the Core Diet. Two thirds of your daily calories should come from vegetable foods (Including rice, rice products, or other grain alternatives). During the first Phase of the diet, vegetables must are cooked - they are better tolerated than raw. Eat 4-6 portions of cooked vegetables per day. Cooked vegetables can be served cold as well as hot and can be used in "salads". Cooking menas steaming, microwaving, or baking vegetables. To promote easy digestion, mash or puree cooked vegetables. Basic mashed vegetables might include carrots, sweet potato, yams, squash, singly or in combination. Cook the vegetable(s) of your choice, add add a little vegetable oil, mash them and add salt to taste.

P1 Fried Zucchini
Lightly fry thin slices of zucchini in a non-stick pan (or use a small amount of oil) until just browned. Season with salt and/or pepper and serve.

P1 Stuffed Vegetables
Basic Stuffing: Choose one or more of the following: pulp from squash, rice, and any other Phase 1 vegetable, moisten the stuffing, add water or juice from canned pears/peaches to moisten and season the stuffing with your choice of salt, herbs (parsley, oregano, rosemary), or pepper. For summer squash, cut it in half lengthwise and remove the inner pulp. For winter squash, cut off the top and remove the seeds. Precook both summer and winter squash before stuffing them; you can steam the

squash on top of the stove, or bake it in the oven (see directions above). Stuff the squash, then bake it to thoroughly heat it and finish the cooking - about 30 mins at 350F.

How to Cook Winter Squash

Steamed Winter Squash: Put about 1/2" water in the bottom of a pan. If the squash is small enough, it can be steamed whole. If not, slice it open, remove the seeds, and cut it into serving-size chunks, putting these in the water. Sprinkle the squash with salt, then heat the water to boiling; turn the heat down and simmer, covered, until tender, 30-40 mins.

Baked-Steamed Winter Squash: Follow the directions above, but put the squash in an baking dish instead of a saucepan. Cover the pan with a lid or tin foil and bake at 350F for 50-60 mins.

Baked Winter Squash: Slice the squash into pieces, remove the seeds, and arrange the pieces in a baking dish. Baste them with a small amount of oil and bake at 350F for 40-60 mins, depending on the size of the pieces. Baste every 10-15 mins for to add moisture and flavor. You can also baste a whole squash with oil; bake it until it is fork-tender and carve it to serve.

How to Cook Spaghetti Squash

To Microwave: Wash the squash, then stab it with a paring knife or fork several times all over (so it will not explode when it is cooked). Put it in the microwave (place it on a paper towel if desired); cook on high heat 15-17 mins until soft. Let it rest for 10 mins (either cover it in foil or leave it in the microwave). Cut the squash in half and remove the center pulp and seeds. The flesh of the squash separates into strings. With a fork, carefully lift out the "spaghetti" strings. Serve them as you would noodles. The squash may be cooked in advance; reheat the strings just prior to serving. A medium-sized squash serves 6.

To Boil: Boil the squash whole (or, if it is too big, cut it in half). Remove the center pulp and seeds, and gently remove the strings with a fork to serve.

Sauteed Summer Squash: Wash a summer squash (eg. crookneck) and cut it into thin slices. Saute these in a non-stick pan (or use a small amount of oil) 3-4 mins, cover, and turn the heat down for 1-2 mins. There is usually sufficient water from the squash to finish cooking by steaming (if there is not enough, add some). Salt to taste.

Carrots and Parsley: Steam or microwave carrots and sprinkle them with parsley.

Stir-fried Carrots: Wash, peel, and slice carrots. Stir-fry the slices for 3-4 mins. Add a couple of tbsps water, cover, and turn the heat down to moderately low. Cook about 6 mins. Salt to taste.

Stir-fried Green Beans: Use either tender whole beans or cut up larger beans. Stir-fry in a non-stick pan (or use a small amount of oil) for 4-5 mins, then cover and steam until the beans are bright green and just tender. Add salt to taste.

Basic Stir-fried Mixed Vegetables

1 tsp safflower oil (optional)   2 large zucchini, sliced
1 cup small broccoli flowerets   2 medium carrots, sliced
                                        1 tbsp chopped fresh basil

Heat a very large nonstick pan or wok with the oil, avoiding smoking or bubbling. Add all the vegetables and stir-fry until just tender (stir frequently to prevent sticking). Season with basil.

Deep-fried Yams

Wash yams (or use sweet potatoes) and cut them into thin slices. Fry the slices in oil. Once they are soft and lightly browned, drain them and pat them dry with paper towel. Sprinkle them with salt and serve.

3.2.1 Salads

Only cooked vegetables are eaten in Phase 1 because if you have major digestive difficulties, you may not tolerate raw vegetables. However, it is possible to make salads using cooked vegetables, as the recipes below illustrate.

Vary your salads by adding cooked chicken or turkey, cubed canned peaches or pears, and safe herbs.

Basic Cooked Vegetable Salad: Select cooked vegetables of your choice (eg. carrots, beans, peas). Cook the diced vegetables (steam or boil) and cool by running the vegetables under cold water in a colander if you are in a hurry. Refrigerate the vegetables (if you have time) and toss the salad with a simple oli-water and flavoring herb dressing just prior to serving.

Basic Rice Salad: Blend 1 1/2 cups cooked white rice, oil and water dressing, and cooked vegetables of your choice (eg. peas, carrots). Add dressing and toss. Cover tightly and refrigerate at least 2 hours, stirring once during this time.

Basic Chicken Noodle Salad: Pour boiling water over rice noodles and let stand 10 mins. Drain and pour a little safe oil and water dressing with parsley over the noodles. Mix to coat. Set aside. Cook a few sliced carrots and peas; add to the noodles and mix to marinate. Refrigerate. To serve, top with chopped cooked chicken and a little more dressing.

Variations: Use other safe vegetables (eg. zucchini, broccoli)...add other safe herbs.

Basic Oil and Water Dressing
1 tbsp oil
3 tbsp water
Use safflower, olive, sunflower, or linseed oil. Refrigerate. Shake the dressing vigorously before using.

Create your own variations on this dressing by adding any of the following to taste: purreed peaches, safe herbs (rosemary, thyme, oregano, basil, parsley), salt, and/or pepper.

Basic Croutons

Rice cakes, crumbled	pepper
safe margarine, or oil	oregano
salt	basil

Preheat oven to 350 degrees. In a bowl combine melted margarine or oil (about 1/2 tsp per 3 rice cakes), and seasonings. Mix well. In a plastic bag place crumbled rice cakes and drizzle seasoning mixture in small amounts while shaking the sealed bag. When well coated place on a cookie sheet and bake for 10 minutes or until browned. Amounts of croutons can be stored for up to a week in a sealed plastic bag. This is convenient to use for salads, vegetable dishes, soups, and stuffing.

Variation: Crushed croutons can be used as a poultry or fish coating for baking and frying. Later variations of the seasonings can be added as you progress through the phases.

3.2.2 Vegetable Sauces

Sauce #1: Simmer carrots in stock; puree this (use a food processor or a blender) and serve. You can substitute your favorite vegetable for the carrots.

Sauce #2: After poaching food, use the poaching liquid for a sauce. First remove the poached food, then reduce the liquid, cooking it over medium-high heat to evaporate some of the water and to concentrate the flavor. Then stir in a pureed vegetable.

Basic Vegetable-Rice Sauce
Puree a cooked vegetable (eg. squash) and cooked rice together. Add water until is is pourable. Flavor the sauce with safe herbs if desired.

3.2.3 Breakfast Ideas

Better breakfast meals involve "real food" in the morning. One of the 2/3's rules suggests more cooked meals should be eaten earlier in the day. Breakfast should be a properly cooked meal. A bowl of cooked rice with 2-3 vegetables (eg. carrots, peas, green beans) is a perfect breakfast. Breakfast can be leftovers from the previous evening's dinner, warmed in the microwave. Why not have soup, salad, or stew in the morning? The constant soup or stew pot simmering on the fire is a centuries-old cooking tradition and has probably provided routine nutrition since cooking was invented.

Here are a variety of Core Program ideas for breakfast:

1. Eat Rice mixed with fruit in the morning.

2. Have vegetable or fruit juices as breakfast foods (see p. 44 or some suggestions on making your own juices). Fruit juices are not nutritionally complete, however, so it may be better to consider them as part of breakfast, rather than the entire meal.

3. If you prefer a morning snack, try rice cakes with jam or jelly, a fruit serving, and a nice cup of hot water.

4. Instead of using milk on your rice cereal, use water or add canned pears and/or peaches with juice. Choose rice puffs in the beginning stages of the Core Diet. Later, rice-based commericial cereals (eg. Rice Chex, Rice Flakes, Rice Krispies) may be tried, but evaluate them carefully as they occassionally cause problems. Another twist that may interest children is to puree peaches or pears and combine with carbonated water and pour this over their breakfast cereal. It gives rice puffs an interesting fizz and pop of its own.

5. Any Phase 1 vegetable dish (see p. 29) may be served for breakfast. It is a good idea to consume vegetable foods at each meal, but some people find they make a "strange" breakfast. Try to change your ideas of what breakfast "should" be and concentrate on eating food that will help nourish your body.

P1 Rice Hot Cereal
1 cup cold water
2 heaping tbsps coarse ground rice
safe jam to taste

Heat the water and rice in a small pan. Cook 3-5 mins. Add jam to taste. Note: Coarse ground rice is available at any health food store that grinds its own rice flour; ask them to grind the rice coarse instead of fine.

P1 Rice Pudding
See p. 43.

Breakfast Rice Cakes
Drizzle hot water over 2 rice cakes, leaving the edges dry and crispy. Chop them into some soft and some crispy pieces. Add diced peaches or pears and juice.

Sweet Yams: Cooked yams (microwaved is most convenient in the morning) with some honey, or a little sugar (about 1 tsp at the most) is a nice warm change from rice. Sometimes peaches and peach/pear juice poured over cold yams leftover from the night before is also tasty.

Quick Congee

1/2 cup of cubed chicken breast	1/4 cup peas
1 cup of cooked rice	1/4 cup copped carrots
	2 cups of water or chicken broth

Mix cooked rice with water or chicken broth, chicken pieces, and some vegetables, boil on high until rice has a porridge like consistency and simmer until flavors are blended (5-10 minutes). Add salt and pepper to taste. Makes a good start to any day !

Cereal breakfasts can be puffed rice, Heinz Infant Rice Cereal, hot rice cereals, or rice-based commercial cereals (eg. Rice Chexs, Rice Flakes, Rice Krispies).

3.3 One Dish Meals

Core Diet cooking begins at a purely functional level and may consist, for example, of a rice (pre-cooked) serving, vegetables, poultry or fish slices, assembled in a dish for quick microwave cooking and fast eating. Frozen vegetables may be be microwave-thawed and cooked, or steamed-cooked and served over a bed of rice. Fresh vegetables can be cleaned, cut and steamed-cooked in a wok with pre-cooked rice mixed in at the last moment to make a Core Diet "goulash".

The idea of one dish meals is to cook and serve the basic foods together in nutritious, satisfying mixtures. If you use microwave dishes or a wok, it is quick and easy to clean up. Often we need simple, quick basic menus for routine meals and Phase 1 meals continue to be popular even with advanced Core Diet meal-planning. The simplest version of basic recipes appear in Phase 1. As you progress through subsequent phases, adding more foods, these basic recipes are modified by adding new food options and flavors, as tolerated.

P1 Chicken Soup

1 chicken breast
2 cups water
1/2 cup carrots, cubed/sliced
1/2 cup broccoli, chopped

1/2 cup squash, sliced in thin wedges
1/2 cup cooked rice
salt to taste
pepper to taste
1/4 tsp safflower oil

Cut the chicken into bite-sized pieces. Saute the chicken in the oil until browned. Add the water. Boil on medium heat for 10 mins. Stir in the broccoli, carrots, and squash. Simmer until the vegetables are tender. Add the rice. Season to taste.

Variations: Slow-cook the soup over 2 hours...add safe herbs to taste (eg. thyme, basil).

P1 Chicken Hot Pot

3/4 cup chicken
1 cup rice
1/4 cup chopped carrots
1/4 cup peas

1 1/2 cups water
salt to taste
1/4 tsp oil

Heat the oil on high until it is semi-transparent. Brown the meat. Add the carrots, peas, rice, and water. Stir and bring to a boil. Simmer, covered, for 20 mins or until water is absorbed. Add salt to taste.

Variations: Substitute turkey for the chicken...add 1/4 cup peas.

P1 Fried Rice

4 cups cooked rice	1/4 cup frozen peas
1/4 cup cooked diced poultry	1/4 cup broccoli
1 small carrot	salt to taste

Heat a large non-stick frying pan (or oil in wok). Fry carrots for 2 mins. Add chicken or turkey. Stir in rice and peas. Season with salt. Cook, stirring often, until rice is browned.

P1 Mihoen

2 cups cooked rice vermicelli	salt to taste
1/2 cup diced chicken	1/2 cup diced carrots
oil	1/2 cup frozen peas

In a wok, saute the chicken in a small amount of safe oil. Add the carrots and salt to taste. Add the vermicelli and peas to the wok, mixing well until everything is warmed. Serve immediately.

Variations: Add sliced green beans, chopped broccoli, and/or diced zucchini along with or instead of the carrots...delete the peas from the recipe..brown pear juice along with the chicken to create a sweet sauce.

P1 Chinese Saute

1/2 cup chopped broccoli	1 Tbsp Safflower oil
1/2 cup thinly sliced carrots	1/2 tsp Oregano
1/2 cup french cut green beans	1/2 tsp Parsley
1/4 cup diced cooked squash	1/2 tsp Basil
1/4 cup diced zucchini	1 cup cooked rice
1/4 cup diced chicken breast	Salt and pepper to taste

In a large wok or non-stick frying pan, heat oil on high for 30 seconds. Add chicken breast to oil and stir fry (quickly stir) until pieces are almost cooked. Set aside. On medium heat stir fry broccoli, carrots, green beans adding 1/2 cup of water while stirring. Add squash, zucchini, rice, chicken and spices. Cover to steam the foods until cooked. Keep close watch and add water to keep the steam but not too much that it "drowns" the dish. Salt and pepper to taste. Serves 2 for one dish meal or 4 as a side dish.

P1 Crunchy Chicken dinner

6 plain rice cakes	1/4 cup peas
1 cup carrots - slices	1/4 cup diced chicken breast
1/2 cup broccoli - slices	3/4 tsp Basil
1/2 cup zucchini strips	Dash pepper

Crumble rice cakes on a platter to form a bed. In a large wok or non-stick pan, heat oil and stir-fry on medium high heat, chicken until almost cooked. Add vegetables and Basil. Stir while adding a small amount of water to create steam. Lower heat, cover and simmer until vegetables are cooked. Pour chicken vegetable mixture over bed of rice cakes just before serving or serve individually and let each person mix their own portions.

Variation: Add diced peaches to vegetables just prior to serving and add peach juice instead of water to mixture when steam frying.

3.4 Soups, Stocks, and Appetizers

Soups are very easy to digest, especially when made from pureed vegetables. Soups often taste better the longer they are simmered, so make a large pot and have it on hand for breakfast, lunch, and/or supper. Making a soup
is a good way to use leftovers; poultry meat, cooked vegetables, and/or cooked rice remaining after one meal can be combined to produce a hearty soup for the next day.

Basic Pureed Vegetable Soup

cooked carrots	other cooked safe vegetables
cooked peas	safe herbs, if desired

Place cooked vegetables in a blender and puree (amounts depend on your taste and appetite). Pour into a saucepan, and add water and oil (optional) until desired consistency is achieved. Add herbs and salt to taste. Simmer.

P1 Grain Soup

1 cup rice
4 cups water
1/4 tsp salt

Oil the bottom and sides of the pot. Roast the rice, using a little more oil if desired. Add the salt and water, bring to a boil, and simmer for 40-60 mins.

P1 Squash Soup
2 lb winter squash
water to cover
1 cup or more of water or stock
1 cup or more your choice of carrots, peas, and/or green beans

Scrub the squash well and cut it into small pieces. Cover it with water. Bring to a boil, then simmer until tender. Reserve the cooking liquid (strain it). Peel and mash the squash. Wash and dice the other vegetables you are using. Saute these (do not saute peas). Add the vegetables and reserved liquid to the squash. Add enough water/stock to achieve the desired consistency. Simmer. If you are using peas, these 4-5 mins before serving. Season with salt, basil, and/or pepper.

Yam/Sweet Potato Soup: Substitute 4 medium yams or sweet potatoes for the squash. You can use leftovers: chopped up boiled or baked yams/sweet potatoes or mashed yams/sweet potatoes.

Simmered Turkey Soup
Place boneless turkey breasts in a pot with 2-3 cups of water. Cut up a carrot (or several) in large chunks; these add flavor. Add the carrot to the pot and bring to a boil, then simmer 1-1 1/2 hours. Discard the carrot chunks. Take the meat out of the pot, place it on a plate, and cool it in the fridge. Cool the broth in the fridge and skim the fat off. Cut the meat into small chunks or slivers and add it to the broth. Cube or slice some fresh carrots and add them to the broth. Simmer.

Variations: Add pureed rice to thicken the soup or add a little cooked rice for variety...if you cook a lot of meat, you can use some of the cooked meat for another meal, instead of returning it all to the broth for soup.

Carrot Soup
Cook 2 or more carrots in 1-1 1/2 cups water. When cooked and cooled a little, puree the carrots. Add 2-3 tbsp cooked rice and puree again. Keep adding rice until desired thickness is achieved. Heat and serve.

Quick Turkey Soup: When the basic carrot soup is made, add turkey cubes.

Quick Turkey Soup #2: Cut the carrots and turkey into cubes or grate the carrots and pull the turkey meat into little slivers. Omit the rice.

P1 Chicken and/or Vegetable Stock

1 1/2 L water	1 tsp dried thyme
1 tbsp chopped parsley	1 tsp chopped dried basil
2 cups chopped carrots	1 Kg chicken breasts
	1 tsp salt

Debone the chicken and remove the skin. Combine all ingredients and simmer, covered, for one hour or more (the longer, the better). Strain the stock and refrigerate it overnight. Remove the fat layer the next day. Use this stock for sauces or soups. This can be frozen. For Vegetable Stock, omit the chicken.

"Bouillion" Cubes: Freeze stock in ice cube trays to create ready-to-use "bouillion cubes". You may add grated carrot or rice to the stock before freezing if desired. The cubes can be used for a hot mug of soup or, if used in larger quantities, can be soup starters.

Turkey Skewers: Alternately skewer cubes of roast turkey (white), chunks of canned peach/pear, and cubes of roast turkey (dark) onto toothpicks.

Steamed meatballs

1/2 lb ground chicken or turkey	1 tsp oregano
4 Tbsp cooked rice	1/4 tsp olive oil

In a bowl combine ingredients. Prepare metal or bamboo steamer. One option is to place small heat proof saucers and place peas on the bottom. Form mixture into balls. Place balls on top of peas to prevent sticking to cookware. Steam for 15-20 minutes on medium to high heat. Pepper to taste. Serve hot.

3.5 Entrees

Poultry (chicken and turkey, preferably boneless, skinless, defatted breast meat) is the meat choice for the first week. It is preferable to bake, poach, or microwave poultry. In general, avoid frying, although wok cooking is is alright if you use the lid to steam the food in a little water (see p. 16).

Basic Roast Chicken
Rinse and dry a 3 lb roasting chicken. Put it on a rack in an uncovered roasting pan and roast at 375F for 1 1/2 hrs, or until the juices run clear when a thigh is pricked with a fork. Slice and serve.

Variations: Rub the chicken lightly with salt and pepper prior to roasting...stuff the chicken just prior to roasting with your favorite safe stuffing (see p. 41).

Basic Roast Turkey
Rinse and dry an 8lb turkey. Put it, breast side up, on a large piece of tinfoil in a shallow roasting pan. Seal the foil around the turkey. Roast at 450F for 2 1/4 hrs, opening the foil for the last 1/2 hour to allow the skin to brown and turn crispy. Slice and serve.

Variations: Rub the turkey lightly with salt and pepper prior to roasting...stuff the turkey just prior to roasting with your favorite safe stuffing (see p. 41).

P1 Turkey/Chicken Patties
1/2 lb ground turkey/chicken	salt to taste
1 rice cake, finely crumbled	less than 1/4 cup water/stock

Mix all ingredients (except water) well. Form into round patties and bake in a casserole dish with water/stock. Makes 7 small patties.

P1 Poached Chicken/Turkey Pieces
Put chicken pieces into a saucepan with juice from canned peaches/pears, some safe herbs (eg. parsley and basil), and a little water. Cover and cook until tender. Move chicken pieces to baking dish and broil to brown. The chicken can be served over rice or rice noodles.

Turkey Minute Steak
Cook turkey steak in the microwave until no longer pink or fry it in a non-stick pan. To brown the steak, use a frying pan; pour in some juice from canned peaches/pears. Simmer the juice until it turns brown (continue adding juice until you have enough to coat the steak). Put the steak in the pan and keep turning it until it picks up the brown. This steak can be frozen and reheated.

Stuffed Turkey Minute Steak
Precook carrot sticks, cut into the width of the steak. Precook the steak as above; do not brown. When the steak is cool enough to handle, lay cooked carrot sticks on the middle of the steak. Using string (12"-14"), tie this up in a bundle. In a clean frying pan, brown the steak as above. To serve, lay peach slices on top and heat. Serve on a bed of rice with pear juice gravy.

Variation: This steak can be stuffed with Rice-Peach Stuffing instead of carrots.

Peachy Chicken
1 boneless chicken breast
1 can peach slices, with juice
water

Remove the skin and cube the chicken. Heat the peach juice in a wok or frying pan. Saute the chicken over medium low until tender, about 10 mins. Serve on a bed of rice, topping the cicken with peach slices (warmed in the pan or cold).

Turkey and Vegetables

turkey, white meat (3-6 lbs)   1/4 cup oil
2 cups lightly steamed safe   1/2 tsp oregano
vegetables (eg. carrots and   1/2 tsp basil
peas)   salt to taste

Preheat the oven to 350F. Insert a meat thermometer into the turkey at the thickest part, taking care that it is not touching a bone. Place the turkey on a rack in a shallow roasting pan; mix the oil and spices together to baste it. Roast for 1 1/2-2 1/2 hours (depends on the size of the roast; meat thermometer will register 180F when the turkey is ready). Drain any leftover basting juices and combine this with the vegetables. To serve, arrange the vegetables on a serving plate and place the roast on top.

Quick Casserole
Make a casserole of layered cooked rice, small cubes of turkey and finely chopped cooked carrots. Bake for 1/2 hour or less.

Variations: Brown peach juice and pour this over the casserole before heating...dice peaches and brown them in peach juice, adding these to the top of the casserole before heating.

Carrot Stuffing
When baking a whole chicken, use partially cooked carrot sticks to stuff it. For chicken/turkey steaks, cut the carrot sticks to the same length as the steak.

Rice Stuffing
Substitute cooked rice for bread crumbs in poultry, fish, or meat stuffings. Use in the same quantities as bread crumbs.

Rice-Peach Stuffing
1/2 - 3/4 cup cooked rice
1/2 cup cubed peaches

Mix together and stuff precooked minute steak .

Rice Cereal Coating

Cream of rice (dry) or crushed rice cereal (rice puffs, Rice Krispies, or Rice Flakes) can be used as a coating for poultry or fish (freeze rice puffs before attempting to crush them). Dip the poultry/fish in water or pear juice to help the coating stick. You may wish to season the coating with salt, pepper, and/or safe herbs.

3.6 Tastey Food Ideas

3.6.1 Spreads

Spreads can be used on rice cakes. They can be made from a wide variety of foods. Mash your favorite cooked vegetable (eg. squash, carrots), adding safe herbs and salt if desired, (see recipe examples below) or use Gerber and Heinz Baby or Junior foods as rice cake spreads.

Commercial or homemade jams or jellies without food coloring or preservatives may be used. Pectin is generally a safe ingredient; however, if you encounter problems with it, you can make jam without pectin (see p. 42). Try sugarless peach or pear jam/jelly in Phase 1.

Canned Peach/Pear Spread

Mash canned peaches or pears and spread on rice cakes.

Green Bean Spread

Cook green beans until very tender, then mash them right away. Spread on rice cakes.

Basic Fruit Butter

Pare, core, and dice peaches and/or pears. Simmer the fruit in a saucepan, stirring often to prevent sticking, until mushy. Press the mush through a sieve. Return it to the pan and simmer over low heat to thicken if desired (watch so that it does not burn on the bottom).

Making Jam without Pectin

Put two silver dollars in the pot in which you are making the jam. Stir the jam longer and over lower heat than you would if making jam with pectin.

3.6.2 Seasonings

Light garden herbs (rosemary, thyme, oregano, basil, parsley) and salt (in moderate amounts) may be used for flavoring foods.

Herb Mix

1 tbsp dried oregano	1 tbsp crumbled dried parsley
1 tsp dried rosemary	1 tsp dried thyme
	2 tbsp dried basil

Mix all the ingredients well (grind them into a powder if desired). Store the mix in a jar with a tight-fitting lid.

3.6.3 Snacks, Drinks and Desserts

Snack foods can be made from well-tolerated phase 1 foods. In designing snacks we want to balance safe, biologically-correct food selection against our need for pleasurable and convenient foods. By making your own snack foods you stay in control of the ingredients and quality, and you will do better than risking unknown problems in manufactured foods.

Some simple snack suggestions are: canned peaches/pears, a slice of chicken or turkey, hot or cold rice cereal, rice cakes with/without jam, a blender shake made of safe fruit and juice, deep-fried Rice Cakes (see p. 28)

P1 Fruit Salad
Toss together canned peaches and/or pears, cubed or sliced, and chill.

P1 Rice Hot Cereal
See p. 34.

P1 Rice Pudding
1 1/2 cups cooked rice
1 cup canned peaches and juice
1/2 tsp salt

Combine all the ingredients in a casserole dish and bake for 30 mins in a moderate oven. Serve warm.

Basic Popsicles: Freeze cubes or popsicles of safe fruit juice. Blend pureed fruit with the juice before freezing if desired.

Basic Rice-Fruit Puree: Puree some safe fruit (with juice) and rice together. Place this in a dish and freeze.

P1 Fruit Sherbet
Freezing
You can freeze sherbets using an ice-cream maker, following the manufacturer's instructions. If you do not have an ice-cream maker, freeze the sherbets in ice cube trays or metal cake pans. When partially frozen, puree the ice cubes or beat the pan mixture by hand, then refreeze the sherbet in a covered container prior to serving.

Canned Peach Sherbet: Reserve the syrup from 8 canned peaches. Puree the peaches and mix in the syrup. Freeze as directed above.

A topping may be a sauce or it may be dry (eg. rice cereal). Pour sauces over frozen desserts, puddings, cakes, or dry cereal, or spread them on rice cakes or between cake layers, depending on your taste. Dry toppings can be sprinkled over frozen desserts or puddings.

Pear Sauce
Quarter and core fresh pears. Steam the pieces until tender, then puree them.

3.6.4 Beverages

Water is the principle beverage of the Core Diet; drink it cold, with or without ice, or hot. For variety, make your own juices in a blender/juicer using your favorite safe fruits or vegetables. If you are rushed, buy frozen, unsweetened juices; commercial juices are generally made from raw fruits or vegetables, so introduce them only after you have eaten the fruit/vegetable raw and have encountered no problems.

Basic Vegetable Juices
Wash and peel your raw vegetables carefully.
Puree vegetable(s) of your choice in a blender with enough water to achieve the desired consistency. Use cooked (or in Phase 2 raw) vegetables (cooked are easier to digest). For **basic vegetable juice combos:** blend 2 or more of your favorite safe juices together.

Fruit Spritzer Blend 2 canned peach or pear halves (with juice) in a blender and mix with carbonated or soda water and add ice.
You can freeze the fruit or vegetable purees in an ice-cube tray to add to water as a flavoring cube.

Chapter 4
PHASE 2

4.1 Redesigning Food Pleasures

Our goal in phase 2 is to redesign safe, nourishing, and more pleasing meals. The goal of your menu-planning is to balance food intake between stability of nutrient and energy supply, and taste diversity. You may eat staple foods every day if they are well-tolerated.

During Phase 2 you re-introduce many important foods and develop more interesting varied meals. Meal-planning in Phase 2 becomes the basis of your new long-term eating pattern. Continue to use well-tolerated Phase 1 foods as staples. Phase brings an increase in vegetable and fruit options plus the choice of raw and cooked. Cereal grains are not included and we use rice flour and other grain substitutes for baking. Fish and meat options are suggested, but can be omitted on a vegetarian program. The Core Diet Program tends to work best if you diversify your menus and alternate the safe foods on your list. The best way to alternate your safe foods is to plan a week's menu in advance.

Be sure to set aside proper, formal mealtimes and allow sufficient time to enjoy your meals, chew your food well, and relax after eating. Make a rule that mealtimes are for eating and avoid distractions. In families, mealtime may be the only occasion when everyone is together, providing a good opportunity for relaxed fellowship. Avoid contentious conversation at the dinner table. Food will feel much better to you if you are relaxed and enjoying yourself.

4.2 Meal-Plans

4.2.1 Breakfast

Breakfast ideas vary. Recent suggestions to eat only fruit in the morning may work well for some people and not for others. Fruit is not nutritionally complete, and its high sugar content will often induce sugar cravings. Fruit juices are desirable breakfast foods, but are not always suitable for people with food allergies. The citrus juices and apple juice have not been well-tolerated, in our experience. You can take any fruit that suits you and create homemade juices, using a blender or juicer. Homemade vegetable juices are highly desirable. Raw-food fans advocate only fresh raw juiced vegetables; however, for many people this would produce digestive symptoms and increased allergenic effects. You can make juices from cooked vegetables to reduce allergenicity and still enjoy good nutrition. Cooked vegetables may be pureed in an ordinary blender with water added to achieve the right consistency.

In phase 2 seek well-balanced breakfasts that resemble proper cooked meals. Think of poached rainbow trout, wild rice, carrots, and a sprig of parsley. Many people prefer not to eat a meal in the morning, preferring a morning snack. The continental breakfast of croissants, fruit, and coffee becomes the simplest Core Diet breakfast of rice cakes with jam or jelly, a fruit serving, and a nice cup of hot water (perhaps with a touch of lemon and honey). Cereal breakfasts can continue with puffed rice or millet, and new rice cereals tried - Rice Chexs, Rice Flakes, or Rice Krispies, millet-rice flakes, or hot rice or millet cereals - moisten the cereal with fruit and fruit juice or water instead of milk.

Breakfast Rice Cakes
Drizzle hot water over 2 rice cakes, leaving the edges dry and crispy. Chop them into some soft and some crispy pieces. Add diced peaches or pears and juice.

Basic Brown Rice Cereal
1/2 cup brown rice
1 cup water

Wash the rice and discard the water. Bring 1 cup of water to a boil. Add the rice and simmer until all the water has been absorbed, about 20 mins. Serve with sugar, honey, or fruit.

P2 Rice Hot Cereal
Follow the Phase 1 recipe (p. 34), adding sugar to taste instead of jam.

P2 Brown Rice Flakes Hot Cereal
2 cups cold water
6-8 heaping tbsp brown rice flakes
salt to taste (optional)

Put the water and rice flakes into a medium pot and bring to a boil. Simmer, covered, for 5 mins (watch that it does not boil over). Remove from heat and cool slightly before serving. Serve plain, with sugar, with applesauce, or with 1/4 - 1/2 cup chopped dates.

P2 Pancakes and Waffles
Non-wheat flour pancakes may be disappointing to those expecting the taste and texture of wheat-flour pancakes. The pancake recipes listed in later phases tend to be more satisfactory than those introduced here, as the taste and texture improve with the additional ingredients. The simpler recipes are for those who truly cannot live without pancakes of some sort!

Serve these pancakes with syrups (see p. 48) or with safe jams or fruit butter (see p. 81)

Cooking Non-wheat Flour Pancakes
Use a well-oiled small-base frying pan. Pour the batter into the pan, cover the bottom thinly. Cover the pan with a lid, reduce the heat to low and cook. Loosen the pancake with a knife and tip it out onto a plate.

Rice Flour Pancakes/Waffles
2 cups rice flour
4 tbsp oil

2 tsp baking soda or cream of tartar
about 1 cup of water

Sift together dry ingredients. Add oil and water (you may need to add more as you go). Cook as pancakes or oil a waffle iron and cook as waffles (these turn out better).

Rice Flour Pancakes #2
1 cup rice flour
1 tbsp sugar or honey
1 tsp baking powder

1 tsp baking soda
about 1/2 cup water
1/2 tsp salt
1 tbsp oil

Sift the dry ingredients together a few times. Melt the sugar/honey carefully and mix it with the oil. Add liquids to dry ingredients, using enough water to achieve a pancake batter consistency, and mix. Fry as per Cooking Non-Wheat Flour Pancakes instructions. Note: 1/2 cup of brown rice flour may be substituted for 1/2 cup white rice flour for a different flavor.

Rice Flour Pancakes #3

3/4 cup rice flour	1/2 tsp salt
1 1/2 tbsp baking powder	oil
1/2 tsp baking soda	juice (apple or pear)

Take 1/4 cup of dry ingredients and add 2 tsp oil and enough juice to make a creamy consistency. Cook in a heavy pan with a little oil. Makes 7-8 pancakes.

Syrups

Basic Fruit Syrup

Use safe fresh or frozen fruits. Wash, cook, and mash the fruit, then simmer it until thickened. Add a little sugar if desired (1 tbsp sugar to 1 1/2 cups fruit). If it is not thick enough, add rice flour and cook it for few more minutes until it boils.

Quick Syrup

Puree a can of peaches. Use hot or cold.

Sugar Syrup

Melt sugar (watch it as it may burn) or use a commercial pancake syrup that is basically liquid sugar (choose the brand that contains the least potential allergens and evaluate it carefully, as you would any other food).

4.2.2 Lunches

Lunch should be based, if possible, on dinner menus - a full-course cooked meal is preferred. Often we require a lunch to take to work or school. A Core Diet soup, a salad, and rice cakes can easily prepared at home and taken with you. Lunch away from home may be cold chicken/turkey, salad (if you keep the dressing separate until you eat it, the salad remains crisper), carrot sticks, rice cakes with a spread or jam, fruit, or any other relatively non-perishable food. Buy a proper cooked-food thermos and use it to bring along hot soup, stew, or even leftover casserole. Heat the food until it is very warm, then heat the inside of the thermos with boiling water (warm the lid too). Fill the warm thermos; the contents will stay relatively warm until lunchtime. If you have access to a microwave, simply place leftovers in microwavable containers and heat them when you are ready to eat lunch.

4.2.3 Dinner Menus

Dinner at home is generally the least difficult meal to create. A simple meal plan would begin with the choice of:

  * A rice portion
  * Cooked vegetables - choose a mixture of 3 or 4
  * Salad vegetables - choose a mixture of 2 or 3
  * A poultry, fish, or meat portion

Vegetables can be chosen by their average nutritive properties. For example, choose four cooked vegetables using the following criteria:

1. One yellow-orange vegetable (tends to have a higher caloric value and is more filling) - yams, sweet potatoes, winter squash, carrots, and turnips.

2. One legume - we begin with cooked peas and green beans, and later include dried beans, lentils, and split peas.

3. One Brassica vegetable - broccoli, cauliflower, cabbage, and Brussels sprouts.

4. One (leafy) green vegetable - lettuce, bok choy, spinach, and beet greens.

Flavoring is best achieved with simple culinary herbs. Initially we avoid ginger, mustard, garlic, onion, cinnamon, nutmeg, cayenne, cloves, chili, paprika, and curry, since these are potent spices with drug-like effects, and many people have problems with them. In the beginning of Core Diet cooking, it is advisable to keep your food simple. Later, very slowly, add more flavors to your meals, one at a time, and assess first the effect on your palate and, later, on the rest of your body. Traditional recipes can be adapted to the Core Diet with substitutions for the disallowed ingredients.

Experiment with new food combinations. Your kitchen is the laboratory where you brew up body chemistry. If one experiment does not work, change the formula and try again.

4.3 Profiles of Phase 2 Foods

4.3.1 Rice Varieties

New rice varieties are introduced in Phase 2, beginning with the different types of ordinary white rice. It comes in long- or short-grain varieties. Long-grain rice is easier to cook (oval-grained rice does not boil as well as it steams). Long-grain rice can be used for boiling, or in recipes calling for rice. Short-grain rice is best for puddings. Try cooking them as directed in Phase 1; note that converted rice generally takes a little longer to cook than other types of white rice. Brown and Basmati rice have nuttier flavors. Brown Rice is hulled rice and can be treated like long-grain rice, but requires more time to cook. Basmati Rice should be washed and soaked before use. Glutinous Rice (or sweet sticky rice) is harder to digest. Its texture makes it perfect for puddings and other desserts. (Note: wild rice is not really a rice, but a seed of an aquatic grass). Rice polish (the bran from hulled rice) is used in some recipes.

4.3.2 Vegetables

Vegetables are once again an important food. All the cooked vegetables from Phase 1 that were well-tolerated may now be tried raw. Introduce the Phase 2 vegetables following the same policy of cooked first, then raw if well-tolerated.

Asparagus is a member of the Lily family (Liliaceae), asparagus officinalis. It is low in calories and carbohydrates. 1 cup contains more protein (3-6 g) than 1 cup cooked rice (3-5 g). The green stalks are much better sources of vitamin A than the white. Asparagus is a fair source of thiamin, riboflavin, and niacin. Fresh, frozen, and canned asparagus have different textures and flavors.

Brussels Sprouts are Brassica oleracea, variety gemmifera. They are closely related to the cabbage and contain goiterogenic substances. They are almost 90% water and are low in calories (50-60 Kcal per cup). 1 cup of cooked Brussels sprouts provides 5 g protein, about the same as from 1 cup of cooked rice, but with only 1/3 the calories. Their phosphorus content is more than double their calcium content, so other foods with more favorable calcium-potassium ratios should be consumed with them. They are a fair to good source of iron and an excellent source of potassium. They contain moderate amounts of vitamin A and are rich in vitamin C. When overcooked, Brussels sprouts become mushy and have an strong odor resembling cabbage.

Cauliflower is Brassica oleracea, variety botrytis, derived from the wild cabbage. It is a member of the mustard family (Cruciferae). Members of this family contain small amounts of goiter-causing (goitrogenic) substances. Cauliflower is low in calories (23-32 Kcal per cup) and high in water (over 90%). Blanching cauliflower reduces its vitamin A content compared to most of the other cabbage vegetables; however, the purple-headed varieties which turn green when cooked contain much more vitamin A. 1 cup cooked cauliflower provides about the same vitamin C as a medium orange; raw cauliflower provides at least 20% more than cooked. Cauliflower should be well-cooked to denature goitrogens and gas-producing substances.

Celery (Apium graveolens, variety dulce) is a member of the parsley family (Umbelliferae), related to caraway, carrots, celerica, dill, fennel, parsley, and parsnips. Its botanical name is Apium graveolens, variety dulce. The stalks have a high water content (94%) and a low caloric content (17 Kcal per 100 g). They are an excellent source of potassium and a fair source of vitamins A and C, with a lower vitamin A content in white varieties and blanched green celery. The leaves are much richer in calcium, iron, potassium, and vitamins A and C than the stalks. Wash celery well to remove the dirt at the base.

Cucumber (Cucumis sativus) belongs to the gourd or melon family (Cucurbitaceae), which also includes pumpkins and squash. Cucumbers have a very high water content (95%) and are low in calories (15 Kcal per 100 g). They are also low in most nutrients, but are a fair source of iron, potassium, and vitamins A and C (most of the vitamin A is in the rind, so peeled cucumbers contain only traces of vitamin A). Be sure to remove the peel of store-bought cucumbers as they are waxed.

Lettuce is a member of the sunflower family (Compositae), Lactuca sativa. The four main types are Crisp-headed (Iceberg), Butterhead, Romaine, and Looseleaf. Lettuce has a high water content (94-96%) and is low in calories (13-18 Kcal/100 g). The darker the green color, the richer the lettuce is likely to be in nutrients (ie. Butterhead, Looseleaf, and Romaine contain significantly more iron and vitamin A than Iceberg lettuce). Romaine contains about 10 times more folic acid than the other types. To store lettuce, wash it and dry it thoroughly (a salad spinner/dryer is handy for this). Wrap the leaves in paper towel, place this in a plastic bag, and refrigerate. Before washing head lettuce, remove the core.

Onions are members of the lily family (Liliaceae). The onion's botanical name is Allium cepa, (variety cepa is the common onion, variety aggregatum is the shallot). The most pungent varieties keep the best in storage because the pungency is due to a component that acts as a preservative. Onions also have a mild antibacterial effect and contain adenosine. The use of excessive amounts of either dehydrated onions or onion powder may result in a strong laxative effect and irritation of the GI tract, because these products are highly concentrated sources of the irritants present in fresh onions. Dry, mature onions are high in water content and low in calories, protein, and most other nutrients. They are a fair source of potassium. They contain barely enough vitamin C to prevent scurvy (about 10 mg/100 g). As well as trying onions, you may try green onions and chives in this Phase. Green Onions (immature) have leafy tops which are nutritionally superior to their bulbs and to mature bulbs. They are a better source of potassium, an excellent source of vitamin A, and a good source of vitamin C. Mature dry onions should be hard, without soft spots or green sprouts. Store them in a cool, dry place. Green onions should be refrigerated. The tearing effect of onions can be reduced by chilling the onion prior to cutting, or by processing the onion under running tap water. Chives are members of the Alliaceae family, Allium schoenoprasum, but differ from other onion plants (genus Allium) in that the edible part is the leaves instead of the bulb. Chives are high in water and low in calories and protein. They are a fair source of calcium, a good source of iron, potassium, and vitamin C, and an excellent source of vitamin A. Cooked chives can be consumed in greater quantities than raw by most people, as much of the pungency is lost in cooking; most of the nutritional value is retained in cooking. Generally, chives are used for their flavor and color.

Spinach, Spinacia oleracea, is a member of the goosefoot family (Chenopodiaceae), and is related to beets, chard, and hardy weeds. It has a high water content (90-93%) and is low in calories. It is an excellent source of magnesium, iron, potassium, and vitamin A, a good source of calcium and vitamin C (only when raw), and a fair to good source of phosphorus, zinc, pantothenic acid, and pyroxidine (vitamin B-6). Considerable amounts of the minerals and vitamins in raw spinach leach into the cooking water, so use a minimum of water and save it for soup bases or sauces. Spinach provides 12.3 g protein per 100 Kcal; ie. significant amounts of dietary protein may be supplied by spinach if sufficiently large quantities are consumed. Spinach contains more than twice as much calcium as phosphorus. Wash spinach repeatedly to remove dirt. Frozen spinach will yield less than it would appear due to all the water it contains.

Turnips (Brassica rapa) belong to the Mustard Family (Cruciferae). There are several different types of turnip roots - carrot-shaped, round, spindly, and flat and broad. Turnip roots are high in water (90-94%) and low in calories (29-53 Kcal per cup). Thus, they supply only about 1/3 the calories of potatoes, although both are considered "starchy" vegetables. Choose smooth, firm, heavy turnips with few scars and roots. Lighter large turnips are most likely woody. Pare turnips before using them. They can be eaten cooked or raw.

4.3.3 Fruit

Several fruit options are tried in Phase 2. The order of introduction, based on tolerance levels, is cooked fruit first, then (if cooked was safe) raw fruit, then (if raw was safe) fruit juice, then (if juice was safe) dried fruit (introduced last, in Phase 4). Unfortunately, we observe many problems with fruit re-introduction in both children and adults. Allergic reactions are common, often with behavioral disturbances, sugar cravings, increased frequency of urination and bedwetting in children. Children often compulsively drink fruit juice. To avoid this problem, reduce their intake of the actual juice by adding water (regular or carbonated), and alternate fruit choices (see p. 86 for recipe ideas). Preservative-free jams made of fruits you find safe are appropriate spreads for rice cakes and rice bread now.

Apples are pomes, Malus pumila, and are closely related to the pear and quince. Each 100 g contains about 60 Kcal of energy, derived from natural sugars. The apple's flavor is due to sugars and a small amount of organic acids. Apples contain minor amounts of minerals and vitamins. For cooking, use tart apples. For eating, choose firm, juicy varieties.

Avocados are Persea americana. They are fruits. They have a fat content of 11-25%, and, therefore, contain 128-233 Kcal per 100 g (no other fruit has as high an energy value). Per 100 g, avocados supply 1-2 g protein, 500-700 mg potassium, and 300-400 IU of vitamin A. Ripe avocados are soft, but not mushy (to ripen an avocado, leave it in a dark place for a day or two).

Blueberries belong to the family Ericaceae, which also includes bilberries, cranberries, and huckleberries. Their color is due mainly to anthocyanin pigments (bioflavonoids). Raw and unsweetened frozen berries supply moderate amounts of calories (about 60 Kcal per 100 g) and carbohydrates (14-15%), are good sources of fiber, iron, and bioflavonoids, and are fair to good sources of potassium and vitamin C. Sweetened frozen blueberries contain nearly double the levels of calories and carbohydrates in raw and unsweetened frozen berries. Check berry firmness when buying fresh ones.

Melons are the fruit of several closely related plants of the Cucurbit family (Cucurbitaceae) which includes cucumbers, pumpkins, squash, watermelons, and gourds. Types of melons include summer melons (muskmelons, cantaloupes), winter melons (casaba, Honeydew, Crenshaw, and Persian melons) and watermelons. All are quite similar in nutritional value. They contain only about 30 Kcal/100 g and are about 90% water. Melons are good sources of potassium, vitamin C, and vitamin A (when the flesh is deep orange). Cantaloupes sold in North America are actually muskmelons, Cucumis melo, variety reticulatus. Cantaloupes are 6-8% sugar with a water content of about 90%, providing 30 Kcal/100 g. They are an excellent source of vitamin A (about 3400 IU/100 g). Watermelon is Citrullus vulgaris and is related to the pumpkin, squash, muskmelon ("cantaloupe"), and cucumber. It contains about 93% water and only 26 Kcal/100 g derived from its carbohydrates (6-12%). Vitamin A is present in significant amounts, about 590 IU/100 g. A whole ripe melon will keep for about a week in the refrigerator. If you cut the melon, wrap it and leave the seeds in to retain moisture; it will keep for 2-4 days.

Dates are available in fresh or dried form. It is best to reserve introduction of all dried fruit until Phase 4. Dates are high in sugar (60% in fresh, 70% in dried). They also contain some Vitamin A, B-1, and B-2, as well as nicotinic acid.

Peaches are 89% water. 100 g contain 38 Kcal of energy, 202 mg potassium, 1330 IU vitamin A, and 1 mg sodium. Their calories are primarily from natural sugars. Choose soft-fleshed peaches. To cook peaches, broil, bake, or poach them (especially if they are hard).

Pears are 83% water. 100 g provides 61 Kcal of energy, 130 mg potassium, and 2 mg sodium. The calories are primarily from their sugars. A pear should be soft, but not mushy. Pears can be poached, baked, and sauteed.

Plums are drupes, Prunus, and are close relatives of the apricot, almond, cherry, and peach. Plums are 78-87% water. Per 100 g, plums provide 48-75 Kcal (derived primarily from carbohydrates), 170-299 mg potassium, 250-300 IU of vitamin A, and 1-2 mg sodium. Plums should be soft, but not mushy (blue-black prune plums are generally firmer than other varieties).

Raspberries are members of the Rosaceae family, Rubus. They are similar to blackberries, except the raspberry core remains on the plant when picked, while the blackberry core comes off with the fruit. Both are classified as aggregate fruits (each berry is made up of many tiny drupes or druplets, each of which is considered to be a fruit). Black and purple raspberries have similar characteristics, which differ somewhat from those of red and yellow. Their color is due mainly to anthocyanin pigments (bioflavonoids). Raw raspberries are moderately high in calories (57 Kcal/100 g for red and 73 Kcal/100 g for black) and carbohydrates (14% for red and 16% for black). They are rich in fiber, and a fair to good source of potassium, iron, vitamin C, and bioflavonoids. Frozen sweetened raspberries contain about 50% more calories and carbohydrates than raw.

Strawberries are members of the Rosaceae family, Fragaria. They are not true berries because the seeds are carried on the outside of the fleshy part of the fruit rather than being enclosed in it. Their red color is due mainly to the anthocyanin pigment pelargonidin 3-monoglucoside (a bioflavonoid). Raw and frozen unsweetened strawberries are fairly low in calories (37 Kcal/100 g) and carbohydrates (8%). They are a good sources of fiber, potassium, iron, vitamin C, and bioflavonoids. Frozen sweetened strawberries contain about three times the caloric and carbohydrate levels of raw and frozen unsweetened, but levels of the other nutrients are similar. Strawberries should be soft, but not mushy.

4.3.4 Fish

Fish is introduced in Phase 2. Whitefish is introduced first. Fish, and seafood in general, contain complete protein; most contain 18-20% protein, 85-95% of which is digestible. Whitefish are lean, containing less than 100 Kcal/100 g. Fish and seafood are rich in vitamins; the fat is rich in vitamins A, D, and K - an average serving provides 10% of the daily adult vitamin A requirement and 50% of the vitamin D requirement. Fish and seafood contain B complex vitamins; a serving of lean fish yields about 10% of the thiamin, 15% of the riboflavin, and 50% of the niacin required each day. The minerals most common in fish are iodine, magnesium, calcium, phosphorus, iron, potassium, copper, and fluoride. The polyunsaturated fatty acids in fish allow them to play a major role in low-cholesterol diets. Fish is safe for use in low-sodium diets.

Begin with Cod, Halibut, and Sole; later you may try your local whitefish such as red snapper. Note that fish if often the cause of dramatic immediate-type allergic reactions. Atlantic Cod allergy is well-know and studied. We observe significant difference among the fish choices and suggest trying to include fish options in your diet if you have no know immediate-type allergy. Pacific Cod, for example, is not related to Atlantic cod and may not cross-react. Sole has been one the best tolerated and best-liked fish options. Tuna is also introduced in Phase 2. Canned Tuna is usually the most available version of this fish and product quality varies greatly. Some people nbow feel very strogly that Tuna fishing is destructive to sea-mammals and tuna products should be boycotted. Fish may be poached, microwaved, broiled, steamed, stir-fried, deep-fried, baked, grilled, or used in soups, salads, and stews. If you are cooking fish fillets, poach those that break easily, rather than attempting to fry them.

4.3.5 Meat

The Core Diet policy is to reduce the use of red meat options to once or twice a week, if tolerated, and desired. Meat is chosen for low-fat content, and bones are not used for soup-bases. No organ meat is suggested on the Core Diet. Meat is not emphasized in menu planning and meat portion sizes are reduced. Meat can be excluded completely without any loss of nutritionally adequacy on the Core Diet.

Meat options include beef and lamb (or venison for those who do not enjoy lamb). Beef (muscle meat) provides high quality animal protein containing amino acids in proportions similar to human protein. It is a good source of several minerals, but it is an especially rich source of iron, phosphorus, copper, and zinc. It is a good source of vitamin A and the B vitamins (B-12, B-6, niacin, pantothenic acid, and thiamin). The amount of calories it contains depends largely on the fat content. Lamb is the flesh of young sheep, mutton that of mature sheep; the difference is in tenderness and flavor. Lamb is an source of high quality protein. The fat is easily separated from the lean so the calories in a piece of lamb are easily adjusted by removing the fat. Lamb is one of the best sources of iron. It is also rich in phosphorus, vitamin B-12, vitamin B-6, biotin, niacin, pantothenic acid, and thiamin.

Choose only the leaner cuts of meat and use cooking teqniques that allow you to discard melted fat. Meat may be microwaved (although it does not brown as in a conventional oven), roasted, broiled, stir-fried, grilled, or used in soups, stews, and salads.

All meat options can be omitted to create a vegetarian version of the Core Diet.

4.4 One Dish Meals

Often we need simple, quick basic menus for routine meals. Core Diet cooking is purely functional and may consist, for example, of frozen vegetables, poultry or fish slices, assembled in a dish for quick microwave cooking and fast eating.

One dish meals can easily be prepared by quick-sauteeing of poultry or fish pieces in a wok, then adding chopped fresh or frozen vegetables in various combinations, oil, water and cook by steaming with the lid on. Serve on a bed of rice or precooked rice can be added to the mix in the wok to create an "asian goulash". Cooked lean hamburger blended into rice, and added to mixed vegetables is another goulash variation. Fruit added to these rice-vegetable mixes, polynesean-style, adds more variety and taste-appeal.

Variations on "fried rice" can also be complete meals - gently fried cooked-rice with vegetable oil, peas, and apple slices makes a refreshing breakfast. Cook extra rice to save in the fridge to fry with any combination of vegetables, mushrooms, poultry, fish, or meat pieces to make quick meals.

Many people develop the habit of one-dish cooking, especially using a wok to assemble and cook all the ingredients and seldom prepare meals in the old-manner of preparing several "dishes" to assemble on a plate. One dish meals can be eaten from a bowl as well as a plate. Many enjoy the simplicity of a one-dish, one bowl meal with fewer pots and dishes to clean up when its all over. Soups, and casseroles are other routine menu options.

P2 Chicken Hot Pot
Follow the Phase 1 recipe (p. 35) with the following variations.

Variations: Substitute brown or basmati rice for white rice...substitute beef, lamb, or fish for the poultry...add chopped onion or fresh green onion stalks when sauteing the poultry.

P2 Fried Rice
Follow the Phase 1 recipe (see p. 36) and make the following modifications.

<u>Variations</u>: Add 1/2 chopped onion and/or 2 stalks of celery, diced, with the carrots.

P2 Mihoen
Follow the recipe on p. 36 with the following adjustments.

<u>Variations</u>: Saute chopped onion or green onion with the chicken...add to or replace the carrots with chopped cauliflower or diced celery...substitute vermicelli made of rice flour and water for that made of rice and water. Substitute safe fish or beef for the chicken.

P2 Honey Chicken Saute

1/2 tsp safe oil
1/2 lb chicken breast thinly sliced
all vegetables are thinly sliced
1/2 cup asparagus spears
1/2 cup cauliflowerettes

1/4 cup carrots
2 Tbsp honey
1 tsp rice flour
1/2 cup water
cooked rice
(white or a mixture with glutinous)

In a cup mix honey, flour and water into a slurry. Set aside. In a non-stick pan, stir-fry chicken until browned. Remove from pan and set aside. Saute cauliflowerr, asparagus and carrots in pan adding 1-2 tbsp water to steam vegetables. Cover and simmer on low heat for 2 minutes. Add chicken when vegetables are almost done. Make a well in the centre and pour in the slurry. Stir vegetable mixture well, coating ingredients with the sauce that thickens from the slurry and juices. Simmer until sauce thickens. Rice can be added to the dish and combined or the dish can be served on a bed of rice.

<u>Variations:</u> Instead of chicken, any meat will do. Thinly sliced beef works best. Peaches added at the end of the cooking process tastes yummy. Almost any vegetables are suitable for this dish.

Braised Halibut with Greens

1/2 lb Halibut, cubed
1 cup broccoli flowerettes
1 cup zucchini, sliced
1/2 cup carrots, sliced
1 cup fresh spinach

cooked rice
1/2 cup water
1/2 small onion, thinly sliced
1/2 tsp safe oil

In a saucepan, heat oil and saute onion. Add water and bring to a boil. Add halibut, broccoli, and carrots lower heat and simmer covered for 5 minutes making sure pot does not run dry. Add water as needed to keep bottom of pan covered. Add zucchini and spinach. Cover and raise heat to create steam to cook the spinach. Rice can be added at the end or this can be served on a bed of rice. Salt and pepper to taste.

P2 Garden Style Dinner

1/2 cup asparagus spears
1/2 cup brussel sprouts
1/2 cup cauliflowerettes
1/2 cup broccoli
1/2 cup carrots, thinly sliced
1/2 cup french cut green beans
1/2 lb thinly sliced chicken breast

1/4 cup fresh strawberry halves
1/2 tsp oregano
1/2 tsp basil
1/4 tsp rosemary
salt and pepper
cooked rice
1/2 tsp olive oil

In a non-stick pan heat oil and saute chicken until browned. Add 2 tbsp water. Sprinkle spices on chicken and stir. Add vegetables and steam with lid until tender-crisp. Add strawberries when vegetables are cooked. Stir in rice or serve over a bed or rice.

Variations: Any berry fruit is also suitable, raspberries and strawberries taste best. Brown rice or a white and brown rice combination tastes good with this dish.

P2 Cucumber chicken soup

1/2 lb chicken breast (or turkey)
1 cup cubed cucumber
1/2 small onion

1/2 cup winter melon
1/2 cup broccoli
3-4 cups water
2 cups cooked white rice

In a sauce pan brown chicken breast and onion. Add water and bring to a boil. When chicken is tender add winter melon and cucumber. Simmer for 5-10 minutes. Add cooked rice. Serve.

4.5 Cooked Vegetable Dishes

P2 Stuffed Vegetables
Basic Stuffing: In addition to Phase 1 foods (see p. 29), use one or more
of the following:
- pulp from onion to be stuffed
- any safe Phase 2 vegetable
- avocado
- rice bread cubes or crumbs
- apples

Moisten the stuffing with applesauce or honey if desired.

Onions: Wash the onions, but do not remove the skins. Bake the onions at
350F for 25-30 mins. Now remove the skins and cut a slice off the top,
then cut off the root hairs so that the onion has a flat end on which to sit.
Remove most of the inside, leaving 2-3 layers of onion. (Use the center
portion in the stuffing). Stuff and bake at 350F until the onions are fork-
tender, about 30 mins.

Boiled Brussels Sprouts
Brussels sprouts
salted water
salt to taste

Trim off the outer leaves and stems of the Brussels sprouts and soak them
in salted water for 15 mins. In a saucepan, boil a small amount of salted
water. Add the Brussels sprouts and cook for about 10 mins, or until
crispy yet tender (longer for increased digestibility). Drain and season with
salt.

Steamed Yam Casserole

yams   2 tsp oil (optional)
winter squash (optional)   apples
carrots   2 tbsp water

Chop up all the vegetables and the apples. Put them in a saucepan or
baking dish. Add the water and oil (if desired). Sprinkle with salt and/or
safe herbs. Cover and steam, or bake, about 30 mins.

Parsleyed Sweet Potatoes

4 medium sweet potatoes
3 tsp olive oil

1 medium onion, chopped
1/2 tsp salt
1 tbsp minced parsley

Peel the sweet potatoes and cube them. Boil lightly salted water to a boil in a medium saucepan. Add the sweet potatoes, cover, and cook 5-6 mins, until tender but not mushy. Drain. Heat the oil in a large frying pan (or use a non-stick pan). Saute the sweet potatoes, onion, salt, and parsley until the potatoes begin to brown (about 10 mins).

Carrot-Turnip Mush

1 medium onion, chopped
8 medium carrots, peeled
3 small turnips, peeled
1 1/4 cups water

1 tbsp sugar
1/2 tsp salt
dash of pepper
3 tbsp minced parsley

Cut the carrots in 1/2" slices and the turnips in quarters. Cook the onion over moderately high heat in a medium non-stick saucepan (or use a small amount of safe oil) until tender. Add the carrots, turnips, and water. Bring to a boil, then cover and reduce the heat. Simmer for 20-25 mins, until the vegetables are tender. Remove the carrots and turnips and mash them. Put the mush back in the saucepan and add the sugar, salt, and pepper. Stir well and cook, uncovered, about 5 more mins, until the mush thickens somewhat. Sprinkle with parsley and serve.

Glazed Carrots

2 cups cooked carrots
3 tbsp sugar

1/4 cup applesauce
2 tsp oil

Preheat oven to 350F. Combine all the ingredients in a baking dish. Cover and bake 15 mins.

Croquettes

6 small yams, cooked
1/2 tsp salt

rice flour
oil for deep frying

Puree cooked yams, add salt and simmer over low heat until firm enough to form balls. Wet hands and shape the yams into strawberry-sized balls. Roll these in flour and deep-fry them until golden brown (about 60 seconds). Drain and serve.

Variations: Use pureed squash, sweet potatoes, or carrots instead of yams.

Zingy Summer Squash

Thinly slice the onion and the celery. Add the onion to a heated non-stick pan (or use a small amount of oil), stir briefly, then add the celery, cover, and cook for a moment. Add the squash and stir to blend flavors.

Stir-fried Broccoli

Stir-fry onion in a non-stick pan (or use a small amount of oil), then add the broccoli and continue frying for 5-6 mins. Add a little liquid if there is none, cover and steam to finish the cooking, 2 mins or longer. Carrot slices and other vegetables can also be added to the broccoli.

How to Cook Asparagus

Boiled: Lay the asparagus flat in a frying pan (layer if necessary). Just cover them with salted cold water. Bring to a boil, uncovered, and boil until just tender (6-8 mins). The tips f the asparagus will be limp when done.

Steamed: Steam the asparagus upright in a pot (make sure the whole stalk is above water). Steaming takes a little longer than boiling.

Microwaved: Arrange asparagus stalks in a large, flat microwavable container and add about 1/2 cup water. Cover with plastic wrap and cook at full power until desired tenderness is achieved (5-6 mins produces crispy-tender asparagus; you may wish to cook it longer to increase digestibility).

Chilled Asparagus

Chill leftover cooked asparagus, then toss it in a safe oil and water dressing.

Broiled Onion

1 large Spanish or red onion, peeled

Cut the onion in half vertically. Slice the onion halves into 3/4" thick slices, separating them. Place the broiler pan 4" from the heat source. Preheat the broiler. Arrange the onion slices in a single layer and broil them, turning once, for 5-7 mins or until browned at the edges, but still crispy. Serve immediately.

Beans and Onions

2 lbs green beans	olive oil (optional)
sweet onion rings	salt to taste

Wash the beans and trim off the ends. In a large pot, bring a large amount of salted water to a rolling boil. Add the beans slowly, so that the water does not stop boiling. (If it does stop, cover the pot briefly until boiling resumes, then remove the lid again). Boil 10-15 mins. Drain immediately. In a serving bowl, season the green beans with salt and toss with olive oil if desired. Garnish with onion rings.

4.5.1 Salads

Approximately one third of your vegetable foods should be fresh, raw salad or snack vegetables if you can tolerate them. Along with the foods listed in Phase 1, you may now add your choice of the following to salads:
- grated carrots
- diced celery
- diced avocado
- diced apples
- chives
- raw or cooked asparagus
- chopped onions
- tuna

Basic Brown Rice Salad
Add 1/2-3/4 cup pre-cooked, cold brown rice to the salad of your choice (eg. a green salad) and toss. Serve with the creamy dressing of your choice (see p.62).

Basic Tuna Salad

1 can (12 1/2 oz) water-packed chunk light tuna	1 cup diced celery
	1 cup diced carrots
1 small red onion, quartered and thinly sliced	lettuce leaves
	1/2 tsp dried oregano
1/8 cup olive oil	1 tsp dried basil
	1/4 cup water

Drain the tuna. Place it in a medium bowl; using a fork, break it into chunks. Add the onion. Combine the oil, water, basil, and oregano in a small bowl; pour half of the dressing over the tuna mixture and toss gently to blend. Cover and chill for several hours, tossing gently once or twice. In a small bowl, toss the celery and carrot with the remaining dressing. Combine the tuna and vegetables. Serve on a bed of lettuce leaves or place lettuce leaves on rice cakes and put scoops of the tuna mixture on top.

Cauliflower Salad
cauliflower, cooked and cooled, or raw
your choice of grated carrots, celery and/or green onion
parsley

Combine and serve with a safe oil and water dressing.

Carrot Salad #1
Moisten grated carrot with pear juice. Add bits of turkey or safe fruit if desired.

Carrot Salad #2
Moisten grated carrot with an oil and water dressing.

Vegetable Platter
Serve carrot sticks, broccoli and/or cauliflower flowerettes, cucumber slices or sticks, and zucchini sticks on a bed of lettuce leaves. Serve with a creamy dressing if desired (see p. 62).

Stuffed Pears
Place canned pear halves on a bed of lettuce. Fill the centers of each with your favorite safe jam or fruit sauce.

Wilted Spinach Salad
Steam spinach until just wilted, 2-3 mins. Chill. Sprinkle with a little oil or your favorite safe oil and water dressing.

Spinach Salad
1 small/medium bunch spinach
1 large avocado, in thin wedges or chunks
1 large carrot, grated
1 zucchini, sliced/diced

Wash and dry the spinach. Remove the leaves from the stems and tear the leaves into bite-sized pieces. Mix all the ingredients and toss lightly. Serve with a safe oil and water dressing.

4.5.2 Salad Dressings and Dips

A creamy salad dressing can be used as a dip for raw vegetables.

Avocado Dressing
1/2 cup green onion tops, chopped
2 medium avocados
1/8-1/4 tsp salt
3-4 tsp fresh parsley, chopped

Blend all the ingredients well and serve (does not store well). Makes about 1 cup of dressing. Note: this dressing is not recommended for daily use as it has a high fat content.

4.5.3 Vegetable Sauces

Spinach Sauce
Mix fresh chopped spinach with chopped onions and steam or microwave the mixture, just until the spinach wilts. Puree the mixture and season it to taste with your favorite safe herbs.

4.6 Rice Dishes

Different types of rice may be introduced in this Phase (see p. 50 for descriptions of the varieties available). For a change from converted rice, try long-, medium-, or short-grain rice. Brown or Basmati rice are "nuttier" in flavor than white rice. Glutinous rice (also known as sweet sticky rice) may be used in Phase 2; it is suitable for making desserts due to its sticky nature. Rice noodles made from rice flour and water may be tried now as well. Rice paper wrappers (made from rice flour and water) may be used in to make Salad Rolls (see 75).

The basics of cooking rice discussed on p. 26 apply to long-, medium-, and short-grain rice as well as converted rice, although the results will vary due to the different nature of each type of rice. Long-grain rice is easier to cook and boils well. It is good to use in casseroles and other dishes calling for rice. Oval-grained rice is better steamed than boiled. Long-grain rice can be used for boiling, or in recipes calling for rice. Short-grain rice is best for puddings, as it is quite sticky. Experiment to find the type of rice and cooking method that works for you. Below are some recipes for specific types of rice.

How to Microwave Long/Short-Grain Rice

1 cup rice	1/4 tsp safe oil (if desired)
2 cups hot water	1/4 tsp salt

Place the hot water in a 2 qt container. Cover and heat to a boil. Add the rice, salt, and oil (if using). Cover and cook for 11-12 mins. Let stand, covered, before serving.

How to Cook Long-grain Rice
2 cups water
1 cup long-grain rice

1/4 tsp safe oil (optional)
1/4 tsp salt

Boil the water and add the rice, salt, and oil. Cover, reduce the heat to low, and cook 20-25 mins or until all the water is absorbed. Fluff with a fork before serving.

Chinese Rice
2 1/2 cups short- or medium-grain rice
3 cups water
1/4 tsp salt

Bring the rice, water, and salt to a rolling boil in a saucepan. Boil 1-2 mins, then reduce the heat to medium. Cook until small dimples appear on the surface of the rice. Cover, reduce heat to low, and cook for another 10 mins. Remove from heat and let stand for 10 mins. This rice will be somewhat sticky.

Cooking Brown Rice
Brown rice is introduced in Phase 2. Brown rice has a nutty flavor. It is hulled rice and can be treated like long-grain rice, but requires more time to cook. Brown rice flour may also be tried at this time, if no problems were encountered with white rice flour (see p. 76 for recipes). Use brown rice flour in combination with white rice flour to create a different flavor.

Rinse the grain in cold water and drain well. Bring water/stock to a boil. Add the grain slowly, stirring, and add salt (1/4-1/2 tsp per cup of grain). Boil again, then turn the heat down to low. Cook slowly until all the liquid is absorbed (see below for cooking times). If the grain still seems hard or tough, add a little boiling water, cover, and continue cooking. Do not stir it any more than necessary, or it will be gummy.

COOKING TIMES (for 1 cup grain, dry measure)
Brown rice - 3 cups water - 1 hr 15 mins - yield 3 1/2 cups

Variations: Saute the raw grain in oil with chopped onion or celery until the onion/celery is soft, before adding the grain to the boiling water...use herbs and spices (eg. saute rice with chopped onion and parsley; cook as usual)...dice assorted vegetables and cook these along with the grain.

How to Microwave Brown Rice
1 cup brown rice
1 cup hot water

1/4 tsp safe oil (if desired)
1/4 tsp salt

Place the hot water in a 2 qt glass bowl. Cover and bring to a boil. Add the rice, salt, and oil (if using). Heat, covered, for 25 mins. Let stand, covered, before serving.

P2 Rice and Carrots
Follow the Phase 1 rice and carrots recipe and try these variations.

Variations: Substitute celery or onion for the carrot...cooked vegetables from Phase 2 may be stirred into the rice when it has finished cooking.

Risotto

50 mL safe oil	250 mL rice
250 mL chopped onion	750 mL safe chicken stock
250 mL celery	3 mL salt

Saute the onions and celery in the oil (or use a non-stick pan). Add rice, stirring constantly until browned. Add the chicken stock. Pour into an oiled baking dish. Cover and bake at 180C for 45 mins.

Variation: Stir in fresh or frozen peas prior to serving.

Barbecued Rice

1/2 tsp oil	1 cup rice
1 small onion, chopped	2 cups hot safe stock
	1 tsp salt

Saute the onion in the oil until golden brown. Add the rice, stirring well. Add the salt and stock. Place the mixture in a casserole dish and cover. Bake at 350-375F for 30 mins, until the rice is tender. Add more stock if necessary. Toss and serve.

Rice and Spinach

1 tsp safe oil	2 cups safe stock
1 medium onion, chopped	1/2 bunch spinach, chopped
1 cup long grain rice	2 tbsp chopped chives
	1 tbsp chopped parsley

Heat the oil in a frying pan. Add the onion and stir over medium heat until onion is soft, about 2 mins. Add rice and stir until it is coated with oil. Add the stock. Bring to a boil and add the remaining ingredients. Place this mixture into a large casserole dish and bake in a moderate oven for about 25 mins or until the liquid is absorbed and the rice is tender. Stir and serve.

Baked Brown Rice
2 cups brown rice
4 cups boiling water
1/2 tsp salt

Preheat the oven to 350F. Wash the rice, discarding the water. Dry roast the rice in a heavy skillet over medium heat until it is golden colored. Place rice and salt in a casserole dish; pour the boiling water over the rice. Cover the casserole and bake for 1 hour.

"Wild" Rice
1 1/3 cup uncooked brown rice
5 cups stock or water
1 carrot
1 large stalk celery

6 green onions
1/2 tbsp oil
1/4 tsp rosemary
1/4 tsp thyme
1 tsp salt

Dice the celery and carrot. Chop the green onions and saute them in a non-stick saucepan (or use a small amount of extra oil). Add the stock and bring to a boil. Stir in the remaining ingredients. Bring to a boil, cover, reduce heat, and cook until the rice is tender, about 1 hour.

4.7 Soups, Stocks, and Appetizers

Reserve the water used to boil dumplings or vegetables and use this as a soup base. The food boiled in the water will flavor it and may leach nutrients into it.

Basic Meatball Soup
350g lean ground beef
1 tsp rice flour
salt to taste

pepper to taste
1 L safe beef stock
2 tbsp minced parsley

Combine the beef, flour, salt, and pepper in a small bowl. Form the mixture into balls the size of a walnut. Bring the stock to a boil on the stove. Put the meatballs into the stock, stir, cover, and simmer for 10 mins, until the meatballs are cooked. Sprinkle the soup with parsley.

Variations: Add chopped vegetables of your choice to the stock along with the meatballs...add cooked rice to the simmering stock or add rice vermicelli to the soup just prior to serving.

P2 Squash Soup
Follow the Phase 1 recipe (see p. 38), adding the following foods to your list of ingredients to choose from:

1 cup or more of:
- onions (saute first if using)
- spinach (do not saute, add 4-5 mins before serving)
- celery
- greens

P2 Leftover Turkey Soup

2 tbsp chopped onions
1/2 tbsp oil (if necessary)
1 cup diced carrots
1/2 cup diced celery
1 1/2 tbsp safe thickener

salt and safe herbs to taste
1 cup cooked rice or 1/3 cup raw
1 cup cooked turkey breast
6-7 cups Leftover Turkey Stock (p. 68)

Saute the onion in a large non-stick saucepan (or use the oil) until the onion is translucent. Add the carrots and celery, and cook, stirring, 5 more mins. Add the thickener; stirring, cook the mixture for 1 min. Add the stock, herbs, and rice. Bring to a boil, then simmer, partially covered, for about 1 hr. Add the turkey meat, season, and bring to a boil.

P2 Turkey Vegetable Soup

1 large turkey breast
2 1/2 quarts water
3 medium carrots, sliced
2 stalks celery with tops, sliced

1/4 cup rice flour
2 tsp salt
1/4 tsp pepper
1/2 tsp dried basil leaves

Wash the turkey meat, remove the bone, and place the meat in a 6-quart pot. Simmer until tender (2-3 hours). Add remaining ingredients, stirring the flour so it does not clump. Simmer 1/2 hour or longer.

P2 Melon Soup
2 lbs cantaloupe
2 lbs honeydew
2/3 cup water

Pare each melon, remove its seeds, cut it into cubes. Reserve a few cubes and puree the rest, a few at a time, in a blender. Add the water as needed to achieve a smooth consistency. Chill. When the soup is ice-cold, skim off the foam, garnish with reserved melon cubes, and serve immediately. Serves 4.

Variations: Substitute safe fruit juice for the water...use other fruits instead of melon.

P2 Chicken/Turkey Stock
Follow the Phase 1 soup recipe adding 1 stalk celery, chopped, with leaves, and/or 1 small onion, diced, to the cheesecloth if desired. Add all the ingredients except the water to a Dutch oven. Cover tightly and cook for 5 mins over moderately low heat. Add the water. Bring to a boil, reduce the heat, skim off foam, and simmer for 20 mins. Strain the stock, removing as much of the liquid as possible.

Chicken Stew (and Stock)
See p. 70.

Leftover Turkey Stock

leftover turkey breast	2 stalks of celery + leaves, diced
leftover gravy/juices	1/2 cup diced carrots
12 cups water, or enough to cover completely	1 tsp salt, if desired
2 medium onions, coarsely chopped	6 sprigs fresh parsley (or 2 tsp dried parsley)
	1/2 tsp thyme

Combine all the ingredients in a large saucepan (the parsley and thyme may be wrapped in cheesecloth if you wish to remove them easily later) and bring to a boil. Simmer, partially covered, for 2-3 hrs (the longer, the better). Skim off the fat. Remove the meat, shred it, and return it to the pan. Remove the cheesecloth if used. Strain the stock. If desired, puree the remaining vegetables with a cup of stock and reserve this for a soup or a sauce.

4.7.1 Appetizers

Vegetable Platter
See p. 62.

Roast Beef Rolls
Fill a slice of roast beef with a cooked broccoli flowerette, a cooked carrot stick, fresh parsley, a cooked celery stick, or a piece of lettuce. Roll the slice up and spear it with a toothpick.

Stuffed Celery
cooked squash, yam, or sweet potato
safe herb

Mix together and stiffen by adding rice flour. Bring to a boil and cook for several minutes. Stuff celery sticks.

Lettuce Leaf Wrap

1 cup lean ground beef or chicken
1/2 cup finely chopped carrots
1/4 cup finely chopped celery

1/2 cup french cut green beans
1 stick rice vermicelli
4 Tbsp safe oil
1/2 small onion

Wash Iceberg lettuce and separate into large individual leaves. Drain and set aside. In a non- stick pan heat oil and fry dry rice vermicelli until white and puffy. Drain on paper towels and set aside. Remove oil from pan and saute onion and ground meat until browned. Add vegetables and saute until transparent. Pour meat mixture over bed of rice noodles. Each person should take a lettuce leaf and wrap a mixture of noodles and meat (about 1-2 tbsp per leaf) and enjoy !

Variations: small cubes of winter melon or turnips add a flair to this dish.

4.8 Entrees

4.8.1 Poultry and Fish Entrees

P2 Chicken Pangang

1 minced onion
2 tbsp minced parsley

1 Kg chicken breasts
salt to taste
pepper to taste

Mix the onion, parsley, salt, and pepper in a small bowl. Debone and skin each chicken breast then toss each piece in the mixture. Put the chicken in a casserole dish and bake at 350F for 45 mins, or until the chicken is brown.

Chicken a la Ritz

Cut raw chicken meat from breasts into bite-sized pieces. Poach in juice from canned peaches/pears with a pinch of safe herbs. Remove lid to evaporate some liquid if it is too thin. Thicken the juice with rice flour for gravy. Serve over rice.

Chicken a la Ritz Stew
After chicken is cooked as per Chicken a la Ritz recipe (see previous recipe), add carrot, celery, and zucchini chunks, then thicken juice with rice flour for gravy.

Chicken Stew (and Stock)
4-5 lb chicken breast	2 tsp salt
1/2 cup sliced carrots	small onion, chopped
1/2 cup chopped celery	rice flour

Remove the skin, bones, and any visible fat from the chicken. Put the chicken in a large stock pot with enough water to cover it. Add the carrots, celery, onion, and salt. Bring to a boil, then simmer, covered, until the chicken is tender (2 1/2-3 1/2 hours). Thicken the liquid with rice flour to make a gravy to serve. If you are not serving the chicken immediately, refrigerate the chicken and unthickened stock liquid until cool, then remove the chicken meat and skim the fat off the stock. Cover both the stock and chicken and refrigerate separately; keeps 1 day. Or, freeze the chicken and stock together after it has cooled.

Rice Flour Chicken
1/2 cup rice flour	1 1/2 cups sliced carrots
3/4 cup hot water	3/4 cup minced onion
1 1/2 tsp salt	3 cups sliced celery
	3 lb chicken breasts

Debone, skin, and defat the chicken; cut each breast in half. Mix the flour and 1 tsp salt; coat the chicken pieces. Brown them in a hot large non-stick skillet (or use a small amount of oil). Drain off any excess fat. Add the water and 1/2 tsp salt. Cover tightly and simmer 45-60 mins, until chicken is almost tender. Add the vegetables and simmer until they are tender, about 20-30 mins.

Chicken Bits: Cut raw chicken from breast into bite-sized pieces. Dredge in rice flour, parsley, basil, and salt. Saute in a non-stick pan (or use small amount of oil) until cooked through and browned.

Casserole a la Chicken Bits: Make a casserole of cooked rice, diced cooked carrot, green beans, and/or peas, and stock or fruit juice. Put lightly cooked chicken bits on top and bake until the casserole is hot throughout and crispy on top.

Stuffed Chicken Breasts
4 deboned chicken breasts	1/2 small onion, chopped
1 cup fresh spinach, chopped	1 tsp safe margarine

Crushed rice cakes   3 tbsp rice flour
                                             about 1/2 cup water

Preheat oven to 350 degrees Celsius. Pound chicken breasts between 2 pieces of wax paper until tender and slightly thinner. Rub one side of breast with margarine. Set aside. In a small pan heat 2 Tbsp of water on high. When boiling, drop in spinach and onion and braise for 30 seconds. Drain. Take chicken breasts and stuff the margarine coated side with spinach mixture and secure closed with toothpicks. Dip each breast in water and coat well with a mixture of crushed rice cakes and flour. Place on a cookie sheet and bake for 45 minutes turning over the chicken after 20 minutes. To brown chicken better brush lightly with a small amount of safe oil before and during baking.

Fish is first introduced in Phase 2, as whitefish (cod, halibut, sole) and as tuna.

Basic Stuffed Fish

3-5 lb whole whitefish (eg. cod)   1 1/2 cups cooked rice
1/4 cup finely chopped celery   1/4 cup finely chopped onion
                                           1/2 cup other vegetables

Clean the fish and wash it. Brown the onion and celery in a non-stick pan (or use a small amount of oil). Add other vegetables as desired and saute until crispy-tender. Add the rice/millet and a little water to moisten and mix well. Remove from heat and stuff the fish not more than 2/3 full. Skewer the fish closed or sew shut with string. Slit the skin of the fish open a few times on each side. Put the fish on a foil-lined, oiled pan. Bake at 400F until flaky (30-45 mins).

Variation: Use other Phase 2 vegetables. Spinach inside filet of Sole tastes great too !

Basic Tempura

cubes of safe fish   safe vegetables, cubed/sliced
oil for deep frying   non-wheat flour

Coat fish and vegetables lightly in flour. Deep-fry until golden brown. Drain on paper towel and serve.

Tempura Batter #2

1/2 cup rice flour or starch
1/2 cup tapioca starch
1 1/3 cup ice water

Suggestions for tamura dip include sliced yams and squash, chicken breast strips, carrots, broccoli flowerettes, fish strips, and onion rings. Sift dry ingredients together about 3 times. In a small bowl place dry ingredients and make a well in the center. Pour in ice cold water and stir only until dry ingredients are moistened. Do not mix well. Leave it lumpy. Dip in safe ingredients and fry in 1 inch deep oil turning when one side is browned. Drain on paper towels and keep warm in the oven while cooking the rest of the ingredients. The secret to good tempura is to have only a little batter on the food so it is light. All foods that you dip into the batter should be thinly sliced and then dipped so that frying time is minimized and less oil is absorbed into the food.

Basic Steamed Fish
Wash the whitefish under cold running water, drain, and pat dry. Put the fish on a piece of foil. Fill a pot or steamer with water. Bring to a boil and add the fish. Steam until fork-tender (for whole fish, approximately 10-15 mins per 1" thickness; for fish fillet, approximately 4-5 mins per 1/2" thickness). Remove immediately and puree or leave whole. Sprinkle with fresh or dried safe herbs, if desired. Serve hot or chilled.

P2 Poached Fish

1 lb whitefish fillets	1 tbsp chopped parsley
1 medium onion, sliced	1 tsp salt
	dash of pepper

In a 10" skillet, add 1 1/2" water. Add the onion, parsley, salt, and pepper in the water and bring to a boil. Reduce heat and place the fillets in a single layer in the skillet. Simmer until the fish flakes easily (4-6 mins).

4.8.2 Meat Entrees

Beef and lamb are introduced as meat options in Phase 2. Muscle meat (steak, roast, ground beef) is used rather than the organ meat. If meat is desirable and well-tolerated, a meat entree meal can be planned once or twice a week. Choose lean meat options, discard fat, and keep individual portion size less than 3 ounces of meat.

Lamb is an optional red meat introduced in Phase 2; Venison or other game meat may be substituted as red meat, if desired and tolerated.

Basic Beef Stew

3/4 lb chuck, diced	2 stalks celery, diced
1/2 tsp safe oil	2 carrots, chopped
2 cups safe beef broth	1/4 tsp thyme
2 medium yams, diced	1/4 tsp basil
1 small onion, chopped	salt to taste
1/2 cup frozen peas	pepper to taste

Heat the oil and brown the chuck and onion in a large saucepan. When browned on all sides, add the stock, celery, carrots, and seasonings. Bring to a boil and simmer, covered, for 30-45 mins, or until the meat and vegetables are cooked. Add the yams and simmer, covered, another 10 mins. Add the peas and simmer uncovered 5 more mins. If the stew is too runny, thicken with rice flour or simmer uncovered longer to reduce the liquid.

P2 Meatballs

12 oz ground lean beef	3 tbsp minced onion
2 tbsp cooked rice	2 tbsp minced parsley (optional)
2 tsp oil	1/8 tsp pepper

Combine all ingredients and refrigerate for 2-24 hours. Shape into small meatballs. To broil, preheat the broiler, then cook the meatballs, turning to brown all over. To fry on the stove, heat a non-stick skillet and brown the meatballs on all sides.

Fried Beef Patties

1 lb lean ground beef	1 tsp salt
1 small onion, minced	dash of pepper

Combine the ingredients in a large bowl. Make 4 patties (or more, depending on desired thickness). Heat a nonstick pan, then add the patties. Cook uncovered 3 mins per side (or longer, depending on your taste).

Herbed Beef Patties

1 lb ground beef	1/2 tsp dried oregano
2 tbsp minced onion	1/2 tsp dried thyme
1/2 tsp dried basil	1/2 tsp salt
	1/2 tsp pepper

Mix all the ingredients and form into 4 patties. Broil 3 1/2 mins, turn the patties, and broil 3 1/2 mins more (or to taste).

Variations: Substitute 2 sliced and sauted green onions for the minced onion...add 1 tbsp minced parsley.

P2 Roast Lamb
lamb

1-6 lb leg of lamb	1 tsp minced onion
2 tbsp rice flour	1/4 tsp pepper (optional)
3 tsp salt	2 cups cold water

Preheat the oven to 325F. Rinse the lamb with a damp cloth; do not remove fell. Combine salt and pepper; rub all over the meat. Insert a meat thermometer into the thickest part of the lamb, avoiding the bone. Place the lamb on a rack in a foil-lined shallow roasting pan. Roast, uncovered, for 2 1/2-3 hours (the thermometer will read 175F for medium, 180F for well done). Remove the lamb from the pan (keep warm). To make the gravy, pour off 2 tbsp juices and reserve, discarding the rest. Carefully scrape the browned bits off the foil, taking care not to puncture the foil. In a saucepan, blend the reserved juices, scrapings, and flour until smooth. Gradually add the water. Add the onion. Bring to a boil, stirring constantly, then simmer 5 mins.

Herbed Lamb Patties
Follow the Herbed Beef Patties recipe (p. 73) substituting 1 lb ground lamb for the beef. Form into 6 patties and broil for 5 mins (or more to taste) on each side.

Broiled Lamb Chops
Remove fell from the chops. Slash the outer edge of fat diagonally at 1" intervals on each chop. Place the chops on a broiler rack and broil teh chops until brown. Sprinkle the brown side with salt and pepper if desired and turn the chops. Broil until brown. (for chops 1" thick or less, the total cooking time is about 12 mins, increasing by about 5 mins for each 1/2" increase in thickness).

Lamb Meatballs
Follow the P2 Meatballs (p. 73), substituting ground lean lamb for the beef.

4.8.3 Salad Rolls

Lettuce leaves, rice paper wrappers and fresh broad (3-4") rice noodles can also be used to "roll up" a variety of fillings. The rolls may be eaten as is, dipped in sauces, or fried.

Lettuce Leaf Wrap

1 head iceberg lettuce	1/2 cup ground chicken/turkey
1/2 cup finely chopped carrots	1 tsp safe oil
1/2 cup finely chopped green	dash freshly ground pepper
beans	1 tsp crushed fresh basil

Wash the lettuce, keeping the leaves as large (whole) as possible. Set aside to drain. In a frying pan or wok, heat oil on high and saute the poultry. When almost browned, add the carrots, green beans, and onion. Stir while adding the pepper and basil. Lower the heat and simmer until the vegetables are cooked. Drain off the juices. For each person, take a lettuce leaf and put 2 tbsp of the mixture in the center. Wrap the leaf around the mixture and serve.

Variations: Add 1/2 onion or green onion, chopped, with the carrots and beans...substitute ground beef for the poultry...substitute celery for the green beans.

Basic Rice Paper Salad Rolls

rice paper wrappers	rice noodles/vermicelli
cubed chicken or turkey	lettuce
	green onion

Saute the meat. Meanwhile cook the rice noodles as directed on the package. Moisten the rice paper (1-2 sheets per roll-up) in a large bowl of lukewarm water so it is pliable. Carefully drain off the excess water. For each roll: fold the upper third of the rice paper towards you. Place 1-2 lettuce leaves on the paper. Add some rice noodles and some of the meat. Fold the right and left sides of the rice paper into the middle, so that each side covers 1/4 of the filling. Cut the green onion in half and place it on the filling. Roll the rice paper towards you from the top to form the rice paper roll-up.

Variation: Use cubed beef instead of poultry.

Pam's Salad Rolls

2 cups cooked rice vermicelli	1/2 cup ground chicken/turkey
1/3 cup shredded carrots	1/4 cup french-cut green beans

Saute the poultry in a saucepan. Add the carrots and beans. Cook until the vegetables are tender-crisp. Let the mixture cool slightly. In a large bowl, mix the rice vermicelli with the meat mixture. Wrap this into broad rice noodles and serve.

Variations: Saute chopped onions along with the poultry...substitute ground beef for the poultry.

Fried Rolls: Wrap the filling in moistened rice paper wrappers (see instructions p. 75). Fry the rolls in oil until the paper is browned. Serve whole or cut in half.

4.9 Baking

Baking with alternate flours can be a challenge. These flours are more coarse than wheat flour, so they require extra leavening (eg. extra sifting, extra baking powder) to rise. They are also somewhat bitter and may require extra sweetener; adjust recipe amounts to suit your taste. The results you obtain from these recipes may vary depending on the brand of flour you use; if a recipe does not produce the expected result (eg. "hockey puck" muffins), try it again using a different brand of flour. Flours from different stores may be vary widely in taste. Rice flour may be combined with other flours (arrowroot, soy, buckwheat, millet, tapioca) to achieve a better texture in baked products. We usually wait to phase 3 cooking to introduce these flour substitutes. As you try these recipes, you may need to alter recipe amounts as you proceed because different flour brands require more or less liquid. Watch your batter/dough; if it appears too dry, add more liquid ingredients - if it seems too runny, add more dry ingredients.

Baked products made with non-wheat flours require long and slow baking, particularly when made without milk and eggs. Bake these products at a lower temperature as well. Muffins and biscuits made without wheat flour often have a better texture when made in small sizes; using arrowroot flour alone for muffins results in heavy products.

Non-wheat flour baked products tend to be dry and crumbly. Add fruit (eg. canned pears/peaches or applesauce) or vegetables (eg. shredded carrot/zucchini or pureed squash/pumpkin) to a recipe to make the product more moist. Refrigerate non-wheat doughs and batters for 1/2 hour before baking, especially when using rice flour, to prevent hardening. Frost cakes and store them in a closed container to preserve moisture. Freeze non-wheat flour baked products to keep them moist; place them into double plastic bags, wrap a wet tea towel around this, then place this in another bag and seal.

Non-wheat flour breads, especially those made from rice flour, are best toasted. Freeze sliced breads and thaw/toast slices as needed.

Thicken sauces, gravies, etc. by substituting equal amounts of rice flour for wheat flour. Tapioca or arrowroot starch may also be used as thickeners.

Baking Powder Substitutions

Regular baking powder is often satisfactory for Core Program cooking. Commercial products may contain trace amounts of wheat to keep it from sticking and some brands may contain egg and Tapioca starch - if you encounter problems with commercial baking powders, try one of these alternatives:

> 1 part baking soda
> 2 parts cream of tartar
> 2 parts any starch (arrowroot, rice, Tapioca starch, etc.)
> Mix well. Store in covered container.

or *1 tsp* = 1 tsp cream of tartar
     1/2 tsp baking soda
     Add to liquid just before baking.
     Good for breads and muffins.

4.9.1 Rice and Rice Flour Baking

Rice Flour is now an option. Flour can be made from regular rice, raw or parboiled, or may be waxy, having little starch or amylose (essentially amylopectin). It is used primarily as a thickening agent (because rice protein lacks gluten, it is difficult to use for baking). *Rice noodles* made from rice flour and water may be used in Phase 2. *Rice paper wrappers* allow you to make salad rolls (see 75). You may purchase commercial **Rice Bread** made from rice flour and other Phase 2 ingredients (be careful to avoid breads containing ingredients you have not yet encountered). Generally rice bread is best toasted and it usually must be stored in the refrigerator or freezer. Rice flour baking requires the use of *Baking Soda* and *Baking Powder* or hypoallergenic substitutes. Sweeteners are also needed so *Sugar* (including white, brown, and icing sugar) and *Honey* are available. Use them only in moderate amounts as cravings can be triggered by too much sugary food. *Milk-Free Margarine* is derived primarily from vegetable oils, such as corn or safflower oil, and contains no milk products. Avoid margarines which list milk or milk products (eg. whey, curd) in their ingredients. Do not use margarine to saute or fry foods - use vegetable oil instead.

Freeze non-wheat flour baked products to keep them moist; place them into double plastic bags, wrap a wet tea towel around this, then place this into another bag and seal. Freeze breads and loaves already sliced. Thaw/toast slices as needed. If you find the bread/loaf is difficult to slice prior to freezing it, place it in the freezer and slice it when it is almost frozen

4.9.2 Breads

Basic Hamburger and Hot Dog Buns
Use the bread recipe of your choice to make buns.

Hamburger Buns: Oil 2 1/2" deep aluminum foil baking cups. Put about 1/2 cup dough in each cup. Bake 15 mins. Or to create microwaved hamburger buns, use small round microwavable containers and microwave on medium for 2 1/2 mins.

Hot Dog Buns: Make your own baking cups out of heavy aluminum foil. Oil and fill with 1/2 cup dough. Place cups on cookie sheet and bake 15 mins.

Rice Flour Bread

1 cup rice flour	1/2 tsp salt
1 tbsp sugar	2 tbsp oil
3 tsp baking powder	3/4 cup water

Sift together dry ingredients repeatedly. Add the water and oil. Bake in a loaf pan in a moderate oven.

Microwave Rice Bread

1 cup + 2 tbsp rice flour	1/4 cup olive oil
2 round tsp baking powder	1/2 cup water, room
1 tsp sugar	temperature

Mix well. Lightly oil a 4"x6" microwavable dish (sides too) and add the mixture. Microwave on medium for 4 mins. This will have a heavy texture. It slices and toasts well.

Variation: Use white and brown rice flour in equal proportions for a different flavor.

Peachy Rice Bread
Double the recipe for Peachy Rice Muffins (p. 79) and bake as loaves.

Pear Bread

1 3/4 cups rice flour	2 1/2-3 peeled, cored, mashed
1/3 cup oil	pears
3 heaping tsp baking powder	1/2 tsp baking soda
	1/2 cup sugar or 1/4 cup honey
	3/4 tsp salt

Mash pears in a blender or food processor. Sift dry ingredients into a bowl, then add oil and pears. Mix until blended. Pour into a 9"x5" loaf pan. Bake at 350F for 45 mins. Cool for 15 mins, then remove from pan.

4.9.3 Biscuits

Brown Rice Flour Biscuits

3 cups brown rice flour	1/2 tsp salt
1 1/2 tbsp oil	3/4 cup water

Mix the flour and salt, then, using your hands, mix the oil into the dry ingredients. Gradually add enough water to form a dough. Knead gently then shape the dough into balls and flatten them. Bake the biscuits at 350F for 20-25 mins.

4.9.4 Muffins

Peachy Rice Muffins

1/2 cup cooked mashed squash	1/2 cup sugar
2 tsp baking powder	1/4 tsp salt
1/4 cup oil	1 1/4 cups + 2 tbsp rice flour
1/2 tsp baking soda	canned peaches, diced

Blend squash, oil, and sugar; if squash is drier than applesauce consistency, add 1-2 tbsp peach juice and blend. Sift dry ingredients together 3 times. Add liquid ingredients to dry and mix. Spoon batter to 1/2" deep in the bottom of 9 oiled muffin cups. Drop the canned peach pieces on top and cover with remaining batter. Bake at 375F for 20-25 mins. Remove carefully with the tip of a knife as they will split where fruit is and are crumbly. These muffins can be made without adding the peaches. (They do not taste like squash at all!).

Variation #1: 1/2 cup brown rice flour may be substituted for 1/2 cup white rice flour for flavor.

Blueberry Applesauce Muffins: Substitute 1/2 cup applesauce for the mashed squash and frozen blueberries for the canned peaches. These muffins can also be made without the blueberries.

4.9.5 Pies and Treats

Rice Flour Pie Crust
1/4 cup oil
3/4 cup rice flour
1/3 cup water

Preheat the oven to 425F. Mix the oil into flour. Add sufficient water to make a soft dough. Press the dough into an oiled pan. Bake until brown (about 12 mins).

Vegetable Bread Sticks
1/2 cup squash or mashed carrot
1/2 tsp salt

1/2 cup milk-free margarine
1/4 tsp safe herb
1 1/4 cup rice flour

Prepare as per Shortbread recipe. Use more flour if needed. Roll out by hand into sticks about finger-width. Cut into 3" lengths. Bake on an ungreased cookie sheet at 400F 8-13 mins until they start to brown.

Basic Berry Filling
4 cups fresh or thawed berries
1/3 cup honey
4 tbsp rice flour

In a saucepan, combine all the ingredients and simmer. Use in a non-wheat flour pie crust and bake in the oven.

Decorating Frosting
2 cups icing sugar
2-3 tbsp water

Mix the icing sugar and just enough water to make a frosting that can be squeezed through a decorator's tube.

Variation: Color the frosting by using safe fruit juice instead of water (eg. strawberry for pale pink, blueberry for pale blue).

4.10 Pleasures and Treats in Phase 2

4.10.1 Spreads

Spreads can be used as sandwich fillings for rice bread. Rice bread is generally better when toasted; rice bread is often crumbly and difficult to slice thinly so use a toaster oven instead of a regular toaster for better results. Rice cakes are also suitable, as in Phase 1.

You may use safe Phase 2 vegetables to create vegetable spreads. Whenever you encounter a Phase 2 fruit which is safe for you, you may introduce a jam/jelly or fruit butter (see p. 42) made from it. Avoid artificial colors and flavors when purchasing commercial jams and jellies. If you are making a fruit butter and find it too runny, use rice flour to thicken it.

Avocado Spread
Mash a peeled and pitted avocado, season this with salt, and spread.

Guacamole

1 whole avocado, pitted and peeled	1 Tbsp onion, chopped
	1 Tbsp finely chopped celery
	1/2 tsbp pepper

Combine ingredients in a small bowl, mashing avocado while mixing.

Apple Jelly
Wash jars in soapy hot water and rinse well. Place the jars in a pan with a rack on the bottom and cover with hot water. Bring to a boil and boil gently for 15 mins. Cover and let stand in the hot water. Prepare lids as directed by the manufacturer. Heat 4 lbs quartered and cored apples in 5 cups of water to boiling. Reduce heat, cover, and simmer about 20 mins, until the apples are soft. Strain to remove the pulp and then strain the juice through a double cheesecloth. Mix 3 cups of the apple juice with 3 cups sugar in a Dutch oven. Bring to a boil, stirring constantly. Reduce the heat and cook until a candy or jelly thermometer placed in the jelly registers 220F. About 5 mins before the jam is done, remove the jars from the hot water and invert them on a towel to drain. Then remove the jam from the heat and skim off the foam. Immediately pour the jam into the sterilized jars, filling to within 1/2" of the rim. Wipe the jar rims and seal with hot metal lid (the sealing material should be facing the jar rim). Screw the metal band on tightly. Let stand about 8 hours before storing the jars.

4.10.2 Snacks and Desserts

Snack ideas using Phase 2 foods include: serving raw vegetable pieces, vegetable dips, green salads, spreads on rice cakes or rice pancakes, fish appetizers, applesauce, rice bread toast and jam.

Basic Cooked Fruit
Use well-tolerated fruits, water, sugar or honey, and rice flour. Wash, trim, and slice fruits. Simmer with some water (less for more watery fruits). Sweeten to taste. Thicken if necessary with rice flour (dissolve thickener in cold water first).

Basic Fruit Fondue
Sauce:
In a blender, puree 3 pints fresh or thawed frozen raspberries, adding a small amount of sugar if desired. Pour into a serving bowl and place this on a platter. To dip, choose other fruits - peaches slices, strawberries, honeydew or cantaloupe slices. Wash the dipping fruits and cut each into bite-sized chunks. Put the chunks on the platter. To serve, prick fruit with a fork and dip it into the puree.

P2 Fruit Salad
Choose any combination, including those fruits on p. 43 if desired, toss together, and chill:
- diced pears
- peaches, cubed or sliced
- blueberries
- cubed melon (watermelon, honeydew, cantaloupe)
- diced apples
- raspberries
- strawberries, sliced or whole
- sliced plums

Applesauce
Pare, core, and dice 4-5 apples. Place the chunks in a saucepan with a small amount of water. Simmer on low, about 1 hour, until the apple chunks become mushy (add more water if necessary). Add sugar, if desired, in final stages of simmering.

Baked Apples
Preheat the oven to 375F. Core apples and pare the upper half of each. Place them stem up in an ungreased baking dish. Put 1-2 tbsp sugar or honey in each apple. Add enough water to the dish to make it 1/4" deep. Bake uncovered until tender (30-40 mins). You can stuff the apples with different berries with honey or sugar as a great desert.

Pears with Raspberry Sauce
6 large pears
1 pkg (10 oz) frozen raspberries, thawed
1/4 cup water

Preheat the oven to 350F. Pour the water into an ungreased 2 qt casserole dish. Pare, core, and slice the pears. Arrange the pear slices in the casserole dish. Cover and bake until the pears are tender when pierced with a fork, 15-20 mins. Meanwhile, simmer the raspberries in a saucepan to create a sauce. Remove the pears from the oven and drain the water from the dish. Pour the raspberries over the pears; turn the pears to coat them with raspberry sauce. Serve warm or cool the casserole dish, then chill.

Peaches with Raspberry Jam
Heat 1/3 cup safe raspberry jam until melted. Slice 8 peaches in half and remove the pits. Put them in serving bowls and pour the melted jam over the peaches. Serve immediately or refrigerate.

Apple-Avocado Cream
4 apples, peeled, cored, and cut
1 large avocado, peeled and pitted

Blend the fruits in a food processor or blender until creamy, adding up to 1/2 cup of water if necessary for blending.

Apple Dessert
Oil pie plate. Put a thick layer of apple slices on the bottom and sprinkle with sugar or drizzle with honey. Cover with a layer of the batter from the Peachy Rice Muffins recipe, substituting applesauce for the squash. Bake.

Apple Crisp
6-7 apples, peeled, cored and sliced
1 cup rice flour

1 cup Rice Flakes cereal
1 cup sugar
slightly less than 1/2 cup oil

Preheat the oven to 350F. Put the sliced apples in a casserole dish. Mix the rice flour, oil, and sugar together until crumbly. Add the Rice Flakes and mix, breaking them up. Spoon this mixture over the apples and bake for 40 mins.

Peach Rice Cream

3 1/2 tbsp infant creamy rice cereal
3/4 cup cooked rice

3 tbsp sugar
2 cups cold water
canned peaches, diced
1 tsp salt

Microwave the rice cereal, water, salt, and sugar until it is slightly thickened and appears cooked, approximately 10 mins. Add cooked rice and peaches. Heat.

Fruity Dumplings

1 cup glutinous rice flour
1/2 cup chopped fruit (one kind)

(peaches, raspberries etc.)
1/4 cup sugar
water

Start a medium sized pot of water to boil. In a small saucepan, combine sugar and fruit. Simmer on low heat until it reaches a thick consistency. Take off heat and set aside. In a bowl put flour and water gradually while mixing with hands to make a soft pliable dough, not too sticky. Place about 1 Tbsp of dough in floured hands and roll to make a ball. Flatten and place 1 tsp of fruit mixture in centre. Fold over and pinch edges to seal in mixture. Drop dumplings into boiling water until they float. Drain and place on a plate. Roll cooked dumplings in granulated or icing sugar. Serve warm or cold. Great rolled in a mixture of sesame seeds and sugar or for phase 3 roll them in coconut or brown sugar.

HINT: Cooked rice makes a great pudding base. Use glutinous (sticky) rice or short-grain rice for best results, or add extra water to long-grain or converted rice when cooking it, so that it becomes mushier.

P2 Fruit Sherbets

Follow the freezing instructions on p. 44. Some of these sherbets use a syrup base.

Sherbet Syrup

4 cups water
4 cups sugar

Warm the sugar and water in a medium saucepan over low heat. Stir often, until the sugar is dissolved. Cool and refrigerate in a tightly covered containeer (keeps up to two weeks). Makes 4 cups.

Peach Sherbet: Skin 8 ripe peaches (for easy removal, dip them in boiling water for 15-20 seconds, then put them in ice water). Remove the pits and cut the fruit into chunks. Simmer 1 cup Sherbet Syrup gently, then add the peaches and simmer 5 mins. Remove from the heat. When the mixture is cooled, puree it and chill for 1 hr. Freeze as directed above.

Strawberry Sherbet: Puree 6 cups hulled and halved strawberries with 2/3 cup sugar until smooth. Strain to remove the seeds. Freeze as directed above.

4.10.3 Candy and Toppings

Candy is intended as a special treat. While we need and deserve some food rewards high sugar foods may not be as pleasant as we first think. The recipes use a large amount of sugar and may trigger further sugar cravings and compulsive eating.

P2 Puffed Rice Candy
1 cup sugar
2 cups puffed rice
pinch of salt

Melt the sugar in a heavy skillet, stirring until light brown. Add the salt and puffed rice, mixing well. Pour the mixture immediately onto an oiled surface. Roll it out flat with a wet rolling pin, and, when cold, break it into pieces.

Blueberry Sauce
Simmer blueberries until they form a sauce, adding sugar to taste. Serve warm over eg. Peach Rice Cream (see p. 84).

Variations: Use other safe berries instead of blueberries. For example, try strawberries or raspberries...use equal parts raspberries and blueberries.

Raspberry Sauce
Puree raspberries and pour over other fruit (eg. strawberries or peaches).

4.10.4 Beverages

Carrot-Celery-Apple Juice

6 stalks celery

4 medium carrots

5 medium apples

2 tsp honey

Juice the celery, carrots, and apples separately in a juicer. Mix together in a large container and add the honey. Refrigerate. Serve chilled.

Vegetable Cubes: Place diced cucumber, diced carrot, parsley sprigs in the bottom of ice cube trays. Fill the trays partially with water and freeze. Use the cubes in vegetable drinks or in plain water.

Basic Fruit Juice Seltzer

Combine 1/3 safe juice(s) and 2/3 seltzer to a glass.

Basic Fruity Drinks

Pureed and Frozen: Freeze cubes of safe pureed fruit and/or juice (you can use canned peaches/pears and their juice). Add one cube to a mug of hot water for a lightly flavored hot beverage or add several to cold water.

Pureed and Refrigerated: Puree safe fruit and store in a glass jar in the refrigerator. Add 1-2 tbsp to one cup of hot water for a hot drink or to one cup of cold water for a cold beverage.

Watermel on Juice: Prepare 6 cups watermelon chunks. Reserve a few chunks and juice the remainder at high speed in a blender. Put a chunk or two of the reserved watermelon in a glass and fill with the juice.

Canteloupe Cooler: 1 canteloupe

2 cups crushed ice

honey or sugar to taste

Remove seeds and shred 1 canteloupe with a vegetable shredder or slice into strips and puree. In pitcher combine canteloupe (any juices as well) and 2 cups of crushed ice. Sweeten individual servings if necessary. Variations: This is also great as a frozen treat like popsicles if you add less water and freeze or put in ice cube trays and serve with carbonated water.

Chapter 5

PHASE 3

Phase 3 is considered a stabilization period with food additions to improve the taste and variety of menus. We try more flavorings, baking, and cooking techniques to make Core Diet menus more interesting. Wait until you feel quite well and stable before you introduce other flavoring choices. Add new flavors to meals that have worked well before, so that it is relatively easy to determine if the flavorings have any adverse effects. Add one at a time, alternating a flavoring addition with a new food introduction.

The meal-planning and cooking goals in Phase 3 are:

1. To continue eating foods successfully introduced thus far, with the addition of a more flavoring options, more complex recipes, and legumes, as long as they are well tolerated.

2. To practice new cooking techniques - a more vegetarian-style cooking is often the most important new approach. This may involve wok-cooking, experimentation with soups, vegetable stews, rice dishes, salads and homemade salad dressings, rice-arrowroot flour baking, and so on.

3. To develop standard menus for each day of the week. Bigger, better breakfasts and lunches are usually required, using all food choices on the Core Diet. Lunch should become the big meal of the day, although a robust soup, salad, and rice cakes will do.

4. To continue careful self-monitoring, keeping a daily food-intake-symptom journal. You will need to practice monitoring your progress every day, so that if symptoms recur you can identify the cause and correct the problem.

You will likely discover that symptom responses are variable - some foods will prove perfectly safe and acceptable every day in any amount, and other foods will bother you if eaten too much or too often or too fast or in combination with certain other foods. Your body works in a complex manner, and it is your task to tune-in to how you feels so that your decisions about food will produce good results. Note-keeping is a very important part of this self-monitoring, self-education process.

Meal planning with the Core Diet is simple and includes culinary ideas from Asian cooking. At all levels of cooking - for one person or for a whole dinner party - meal planning can be be pleasurable. With additional flavors and food choices, delicious Core Diet meals can entertain guests as well as pleasing yourself and your family.

Steamed rice remains a staple food. You can serve at the table from a rice cooker, or large rice bowl, covered to keep warm or serve individual small bowls of rice at each setting. You may choose to serve individual dishes in bowls or plates on the table. Each person has different food preferences and tolerances and choices on the table are most appropriate. Let each person create their own meal. In Thai cuisine, for example, each person is routinely served white rice on a plate and is then free to choose from a variety of vegetable, fruit, poultry, meat and fish dishes displayed on the table, spooning their choices onto the bed of rice. Individual dishes tend to be eaten one at a time in sequence. In Chinese cuisine, of course, mixed vegetables with added fish, poultry, or meat are combined with sauces and garnishes as single dishes. For routine meals, when you know the tastes and tolerances of the meal participants well-tolerated food mixes can be served as "one-pot" meals. You may present mixed vegetables, with tofu, poutry, or fish and fruit all combined in the wok and presented with a serving spoon at the table. Experiment with eating from bowls with chop-sticks, Asian style - cleanup is then quick and easy.

In phase 3 there are more spices to try that will make meals more interesting. Ginger, garlic, soy sauce, and tofu make a pleasant addition and also give meals a more oriental flair. In cooking with garlic and ginger, it is still wise to keep them in moderate quantities. Stir fry dishes have a wonderful taste with these added at the beginning.

5.1 Foods Introduced

Chickpeas
Kidney Beans
Lentils
Lima Beans
Peanuts
Pinto Beans
Snowpeas
Split Peas
Yellow Wax Beans

Pumpkin Seeds
Sesame Seeds
Sunflower Seeds
Tahini

Tofu
Tofu Products

Tofu Ice Cream

Soy Infant Formula
Soy Milk

Bay Leaves
Carob
Celery Seed
Coconut
Dill
Ginger
Ketchup
Lemon/Lime
Marjoram
Mustard
Soy Sauce
Vanilla
Vinegar

5.1.1 Legumes

Beans, peas, and nuts are legumes, a large category of plants which often have seed-pods. Legumes provide about the same amount of calories as cereal grains, but 2-4 times as much protein. As protein often contributes to delayed pattern food allergy reactions, legume introduction must be carefully monitored. Two legumes (green beans and peas) have been introduced already. Legumes may come in fresh and dried forms. The dried should be soaked for several hours or overnight and the water discarded prior to use; this rids them of some of their gas-producing and potentially allergenic components. Introduce dried Split Peas now. Snow Peas are also an option now (young peas still in the pod, available fresh or frozen). Stew dried beans (eg. Pinto Beans) or peas, or use them in simmered soups to improve their digestibility. Legumes are also good for making spreads.

Chickpeas (or Garbanzo Beans) are rich in calories and contain 20.1% protein and 4.5% fat. Soak chickpeas prior to use. They may then be boiled, fried, or roasted. They are also suitable for salad use.

Yellow Wax Beans have a similar nutritional profiles to that of green beans. Kidney Beans are their dry counterpart. Cooked dried beans generally contain three times as many calories and protein by weight as snap (green or yellow) beans because the latter are 90% water. The dried versions contain three times as much phosphorus as calcium, while the immature versions contain more calcium than phosphorus. Dried and immature beans provide iron and potassium, but immature provide much more Vitamin A and C than dried.

Lentils are rich in calories, proteins, and carbohydrates, but low in fats. They are generally available only in dried form.

Lima Beans are rich in calories and contain 19.7% protein, 64.8% carbohydrate, and 1.1% fat. They are available in immature (fresh or frozen) and dried forms.

Peanuts are rich in calories (343 Kcal per 100g). They contain 25.6% protein and, relative to the other legumes, contain more fat (43.4%) and less carbohydrates (23.4%). Their high fat content makes them undesirable as snack food. Also, overconsumption of peanuts can lead to cravings - anyone who has ever tried to eat just one or two peanuts will know of the recursive looping behavior pattern they can elicit! Instead, use peanuts as additions to stir-fried, vegetable, or rice dishes or salads. They may also be made into sauces; use such sauces sparingly. Peanut butter is a spread option (see p. 120), but, again, use it in moderation to avoid compulsive eating.

5.1.2 Seeds

Seeds are high in protein and fat. Use them sparingly as additions to salads, vegetable, and rice dishes. Seeds may be used raw or roasted. Seed butters may be used in moderation as spreads for rice cakes and rice bread (see p. 120). Tahini is a paste made from sesame seeds and honey and used in Oriental cuisine (see p. 121).

Pumpkin Seeds are obtained from pumpkins, members of the gourd or melon family (Cucurbitaceae), Cucurbita. Pumpkin seeds are very rich in calories (553 Kcal/100 g), protein (29%), iron (11.2 mg/100 g), and phosphorus (1144 mg/100 g). Consumption of as little as 28 g per day will make a significant nutritional contribution to the diet.

Sesame Seeds are about 50% oil (which is oxidation-resistant, allowing sesame oil to keep well) and 25% protein. The protein portion contains a high level of methionine and cystine. Combining sesame protein with soy protein provides nutrition similar to that of casein, the main protein in cow's milk. Sesame seeds can be used to enhance the flavor of vegetable and rice dishes, and baked goods.

Sunflower Seeds of the non-oil seed variety are used for human food. The sunflower is a member of the composite family (Compositae), Helianthus annuus. The protein content of the non-oil seed variety is sufficient to recommend them as a meat substitute (they contain substantially higher amounts of lysine than high-oil varieties). The seeds have 31% more iron than raisins and are a good source of thiamin and niacin.

5.1.3 Soybean Products

Soybeans are a staple food in Asia where they are an important source of protein. Commercial Soy Milk is made by soaking soybeans, then grinding, cooking, and filtering the beans. It is available in plain and flavored versions (check the labels against your safe food list). It is also used to produce Infant Soy Formula. Infant soy formula (eg. i-Soyalac, ProSobee) has the consistency of evaporated milk and can be used in place of it or can be watered down. It is generally less allergenic than soy milk. The curd formed when making soy milk is Tofu. It contains about 53% protein, 26% fat, 17% carbohydrates, and 4% vitamins, minerals, and fiber. Because of tofu's own bland flavor, it can be added to a variety of dishes and will pick up the flavor of the other foods. Tofu can be fried, boiled, steamed, pureed, frozen, and added to vegetables, rice, and fruit dishes. Commercial Tofu Products are increasingly common; check their labels to ensure they are suitable for introduction in Phase 3. Such products may take on fried, dehydrated, or frozen forms (eg. Tofu Ice Cream).

5.1.4 Flavorings

Flavoring options are increased in Phase 3. Herbs and spices such as Bay Leaves, Dill, Celery Seed, and Marjoram can be added in small amounts (1/8 tsp) to various rice, vegetable, poultry, fish, meat, or tofu dishes to impart a subtly different flavor. Ginger, available as powder or fresh ginger root which is sliced for use, has a stronger flavor and is often used in Oriental cuisine. Soy Sauce is also an Oriental flavoring. It is derived by fermenting soybeans and may contain wheat in trace amounts; if this is a problem for you, try tamari which is wheat-free soy sauce. Soy sauce is often rather salty and should be used in moderation. Mustard is available as seeds, dry powdered, or prepared paste. The prepared version contains several ingredients and may pose a problem to you; use it in small quantities (eg. tsps). The same holds true for Ketchup which has several ingredients. Coconut flesh may be used in Phase 3. It is available in fresh form, but flaked dried coconut is more convenient to use. Freeze any unused portions. The coconut may be toasted in the oven or used as is, in moderate amounts. Lemon and Lime juice may be used in tsp quantities in Phase 3. As they are citrus fruits, which are associated with many problems, do not use them for more than subtle flavoring at this time (ie. do not make lemonade or in any other way use more than tsps at a time). Vinegar, a fermented product, may be used in salad dressings, sauces, and baking (it acts as an acid). Vanilla is primarily used in baking, imparting a sweet flavor to products. It is also suitable for flavoring frozen desserts and coconut. Carob is used to give a chocolatey flavor to baked products and beverages. It comes in powder and chip or block form.

5.2 One Dish Meals

The one dish meal concept takes into account the day to day busy - ness of modern lifestyles and the difficulty in staying on a strict diet. They are mostly vegetable dishes with some meat and carbohydrate components added. It is also an assurance that even if you are tired after a long day's work, you can still meet your nutritional requirements with a minimum of work in the kitchen.
Using the Wok as the main cooking utensil reamins a good idea.

P3 Chicken Hot Pot
Follow the Phase 2 recipe (p.55) and try these variations:

Variations: If you are using onions (Phase 2 variation), brown the chicken in thinly sliced ginger root and/or add a dash of sesame seeds...brown the chicken in 1 tsp ketchup or 2 tbsp soy sauce..add 1/4 cup coconut flakes.

P3 Fried Rice
Follow the recipes on p. 36 and 55, using the following suggestions.

Variations: Sprinkle with toasted coconut...saute thinly sliced ginger with the chicken...stir 1/2 tbsp soy sauce or 1 tbsp ketchup with the rice...substitute tofu for the poultry...add snowpeas with the carrots.

P3 Mihoen
Follow the recipes on p.56 with the following modifications.

Variations: Toss in 1/4 cup peanuts or 2 tbsp sesame seeds prior to serving...substitute tofu for the chicken...stir in 1 tbsp ketchup or 1 tsp soy sauce just prior to serving.

P3 Ginger Meat with Seasonal greens

1 Tbsp oil
1 cup snow peas
1/2 cup broccoli flowerettes
1/4 cup french cut wax beans
1/2 cup cauliflowerettes

1/2 cup thinly sliced lean beef or chicken breast
3-4 thin slices of ginger
4 Tbsp soy sauce
1 tsp tapioca starch
1/4 cup water

Crush ginger in a small bowl, add soy sauce and meat. Marinate while prepareing vegetables. In a small cup make a slurry of tapicoa starch and the water. In a non-stick pan, heat oil and brown meat and ginger. Set aside. Stir fry vegetables adding a little water to steam them. When almost cooked, add meat and stir. Add slurry of starch and stir until sauce has thickened a little. Serve with rice.

P3 Peanut tofu with vegetables

1 clove garlic, crushed
1 tsp oil
1 cup firm, pressed tofu
3 Tbsp peanuts, crushed

1/2 cup broccoli
1/4 cup carrots
1/2 cup snow peas
1/2 cup zucchini
1 Tbsp soy sauce

In a non-stick pan, saute garlic in oil. Add vegetables and steam fry until almost done. Add peanuts and tofu and simmer for 5 minutes. Add soy sauce and serve with rice.

P3 Garlic chicken with chick peas and greens

1 Tbsp oil
1/2 cup Chicken breast
2-3 cloves garlic

1/2 cup chick peas
1/2 cup snow peas
1/4 cup carrots

1/2 cup green beans	1/2 cup yellow wax beans

Thinly slice all vegetables for stir frying and cut chicken into bite sized pieces. Crush garlic and mix with chicken in a small bowl. Heat oil and stir fry chicken and garlic. Set aside when browned. Stir fry snow peas, carrots, and beans until almost done. Add chick peas (canned and peeled or otherwise pre-cwooked) and chicken and stir fry until chick peas are tender and chicken is cooked. Serve with rice.

5.3 Breakfast Ideas

In advanced Core Diet menus, soy milk may be an adequate substitute for cow's milk on cereal. A cup of hot water with a touch of lemon and honey is now a beverage option for the morning. As in previous phases, any Phase 3 vegetable dish (see p. 94) may be served for breakfast.

Seed Cereal/Paste
1/2 cup sunflower seeds	1/4 cup pumpkin seeds
1/4 cup sesame seeds	2 tbsp carob powder

Place all ingredients in a blender and blend until well ground. For cereal, serve with fruit juice or water. For paste, add honey and spread paste on rice crackers/bread.

P3 ProSobee Waffles
1 cup ProSobee Ready-to-Use	1 cup rice flour
1/2 tsp salt	1 tbsp sugar
	1 tbsp vegetable oil

Combine all the ingredients, mixing well. Bake in a well-oiled heavy hot waffle iron until browned. These waffles take longer to cook than wheat-flour waffles.

Rice Flour Pancakes #4
1/2 cup tofu	1/4 cup oil
1 tbsp baking powder	1 1/2 cups soy milk + 2 tbsp
1/2 tsp baking soda	vinegar
1 tbsp honey	1/4 tsp salt
2 cups rice flour	

Combine everything but the rice flour until smooth. Add the rice flour and blend until smooth. Cook in a lightly oiled frying pan.

Tofu Puree
Blend tofu with safe fruit and honey.

Creamy Tofu

12 oz tofu	2 tbsp honey
1/4 tsp salt	1/2 tsp vanilla

Blend all the ingredients in a food processor or blender. Serve with fruit or jam.

Tofu French Toast

1 1/2 cups tofu (firm)	2 tbsp oil
1/2 cup water	1/2 tsp salt
1/4 cup honey	rice bread

Blend all ingredients in a blender until smooth. Pour this mixture into a shallow bowl and dip slices of rice bread into it. Fry until brown.

P3 Fruit Salad
See p. 122.

P3 Granola
See p. 122.

5.4 Vegetable Dishes

With the introduction of vinegar in Phase 3, any Phase 1 or 2 cooked vegetable dish tossed with oil and water may now be tossed with a vinaigrette dressing (see dressing recipes p. 98).

Basic Gado Gado

200g green beans	1/2 head of broccoli
4 peeled carrots	1/4 head of cabbage
1/2 peeled cucumber	Peanut Butter Sauce (p. 110)

Slice the green beans, carrots, and cucumber. Chop the broccoli into flowerettes. Shred or chop the cabbage. Cook the vegetables in a small amount of salted water for about 10 mins (or more to taste). Drain the water and use it to make the Peanut Butter Sauce. When the sauce is ready, pour it over the cooked vegetables and serve.

Variation: Add any other safe cooked vegetables to taste.

P3 Stuffed Vegetables

Refer to p. 58, adding any safe Phase 3 vegetable and sunflower seeds to your list of choices for the Basic Stuffing. Vinegar may now be used to moisten the stuffing.

Stuffed Zucchini

6 large, fat zucchini, about 2 lbs	2 tbsps vinegar
2 avocados	1/2 small onion
	1 tsp salt

Trim off the ends of the zucchini; cut the zucchini in half lengthwise. Bring salted water to a boil, then put the halves in 4 mins. Drain them and run them under cold water. Carefully remove the pulp, leaving a shell. Drain the zucchini shells. Drain the pulp in a fine colander or a sieve, then chop it up. Peel the avocados, remove the pits, and chop the avocados or mash them with a fork. Add the avocado to the zucchini pulp. Stir in the remaining ingredients and mix thoroughly. Fill the zucchini shells with the pulp mixture. Chill 1-2 hours, then serve.

Fancy Green Beans

1 lb green beans	vinegar
water	1/2 cup sunflower seeds
	basil

Trim the ends off the beans. French-cut the beans. Heat a non-stick pan, add the green beans and basil, and saute 2 mins. Add a few tbsp water; cover and steam on low for 5 mins. Add a little more water, the vinegar, and the sunflower seeds; cover and steam for 3 mins until tender.

Dilled Carrots

2 cups carrots (6 medium)
1 tbsp fresh dill or 1 1/4 tsp dried dill
pepper to taste

Steam carrots until tender. Sprinkle with dill and season with pepper to taste. Serve with chicken or fish.

Dilled Beans

2 lbs cooked yellow wax beans, chilled
1/2 cup Dill Vinaigrette (see p. 99)

Toss the beans with the vinaigrette.

Stir-fried Cauliflower
Cook cauliflower pieces until just barely tender. Break into small pieces and drain. Stir-fry in a non-stick pan, turning often. Sprinkle with sesame seeds and serve.

Stewed Beans
2 lbs dried pinto beans   2 cups chopped onions
water   1 tbsp oil

Pre-soak the dried beans. Drain the beans, then place them in a microwavable bowl or casserole dish with clean water; cover with plastic wrap and microwave for 8-10 mins, or until boiling. Let stand, covered, for 1 hour. Combine the beans with enough water to cover a 4-6 qt microwavable casserole. Cover and microwave 10-12 mins on high. Stir, then add the onions and oil. Cook for 60-70 mins on medium heat or until the beans are tender, stirring occasionally and adding water to cover as necessary.

Steamed Broccoli
1 head broccoli   1 small onion, diced
1 tbsp olive oil   salt
1 winter squash   pepper to taste

Break the broccoli into flowerets, and steam until tender. Meanwhile, saute the onion in a medium nonstick skillet over moderate heat 5 mins, until tender. Peel and grate the squash and add to the skillet; saute 2 mins, until the squash is just tender. Season with salt and pepper. Gently toss the broccoli with the squash mixture.

5.4.1 Salads

Along with the foods listed in Phase 2 (see p. 61), you may now add sunflower/pumpkin seeds or sesame seeds to your salads.

In Phase 3, vinegar is introduced. Salads may now be dressed with a safe vinaigrette dressing (see recipes p. 98). Use a vinaigrette on any Phase 1 or 2 salads that were tossed in an oil and water dressing.

Marinated Green Bean Salad
In the refrigerator, marinate boiled green beans in a safe oil and vinegar dressing for an hour or more.

Fruit-Vegetable Salad
1 large cucumber   1 medium-sized avocado

2 cups sliced fresh strawberries
2 tbsp vinegar
1/2 tbsp oil

2 tbsp sugar
1/4 tsp salt
1 cup fresh blueberries
2 medium-sized cantaloupes

Peel the cucumber, cut it lengthwise to remove the seeds, then thinly slice the strips. Cut the avocado in half and remove the pit. Peel the avocado and dice it. Mix the cucumber, avocado, and berries together and sprinkle them with the vinegar, oil, sugar, and salt. Toss gently to coat evenly; refrigerate for about an hour. Cut the cantaloupes in half and remove the seeds. Fill the halves with the marinated mixture and chill them briefly before serving.

Cucumber Salad
Peel and thinly slice 1 cucumber per person. Toss with a safe oil and vinegar dressing, sugar, salt, and pepper to taste.

Green and Yellow Salad
1 pound green beans
1-16 oz can chickpeas (garbanzo beans)
1/4 cup chopped onion

Wash, trim, and cut up the green beans then steam them until the are tender. Drain and rinse the chickpeas. Mix the beans, chickpeas, and onion in a serving bowl and toss with your favorite vinaigrette dressing (see recipes p. 98). Chill the salad for 1 hour or more prior to serving.

Rice-Vegetable Medley
1/3 cup finely diced carrots
3/4 cup green beans, chopped
1/4 cup chopped onion
1/4 cup peas
1/4 cup diced celery
3 tbsp minced parsley

2 1/2 cups cooked rice, warm or chilled
1 tbsp olive oil
3 tbsp vinegar
thyme, basil, oregano
salt to taste

Cook the carrots and green beans until they are barely tender, draining immediately. Toss the vegetables and rice together. Combine the oil, vinegar, and a pinch of the seasonings; stir until smooth. Pour the dressing over the salad; toss until everything combined. Chill for several hours.

Long-Grain Brown Rice Salad
1 cup uncooked long-grain brown rice

2 tbsp vinegar
1 tbsp minced red onion

1 carrot, peeled and grated

2 celery stalks, minced
1/2 tbsp olive oil

Prepare the rice as directed on the package (or see <u>Rice Dishes</u>). Remove from the heat and fluff with a fork. Transfer the rice to a large bowl and add the onion, carrot, and celery. Mix gently to combine. Combine the oil and vinegar; toss this with the rice mixture.

Bean Salad

1 lb fresh green beans
1 tbsp olive oil
1 small onion, chopped

1/4 cup minced parsley
2 tbsp vinegar
salt, pepper

Boil the beans. Drain them into a colander, then run them under cold water and drain them again. Mix the salt, pepper, and vinegar, then add the oil and blend well. Add the beans, onion, and parsley; toss. Serve at once or chill.

5.4.2 Salad Dressings and Dips

With the introduction of vinegar, you are now able to make tangy "vinaigrette" dressings. If only small amounts (tsps) are required, you may choose to use lemon juice instead of vinegar. If you are concerned about dietary fat, forgo oil and simply dress raw vegetables with vinegar and herbs.

Basic Oil and Vinegar Dressing

1 tbsp oil

3 tbsp vinegar
1/2 tsp salt

Stir all ingredients together until sugar dissolves. Refrigerate. Shake before using. This recipe can be doubled, tripled, etc.

<u>Variation #1</u>: Add 2 tbsp sugar and stir until the sugar dissolves before refrigerating.

<u>Variation #2</u>: Season the dressing as you did the Basic Oil and Water Dressing (p. 32). You can now add dill, celery seed, or ginger to the basic recipe.

Zesty Dressing

2 tbsp vinegar
1/4 tsp pepper
1/2 tsp basil

1/4 tsp salt, if desired
1/2 tbsp olive oil

Mix all ingredients and toss with the salad; chill before serving.

Simple Vinaigrette Dressing

4 tbsp vinegar	2 tbsp minced parsley
3 tbsp oil	salt to taste

Mix all the ingredients. Chill and shake before using.

Dill Vinaigrette

1/2 cup safflower oil	1/4 cup olive oil
1 tbsp sugar	1 cup vinegar
	1 tbsp dill weed

Place all ingredients in a tightly covered container. Shake well to blend. Refrigerate. Prior to use, shake well. Makes 1 1/2-2 cups.

Sesame Dressing

1/4 cup oil	3 tbsp vinegar
1/4 cup toasted sesame seeds	1/2 tsp salt
	1 cup chopped parsley

Using a blender, blend all the ingredients until fairly smooth. Refrigerate before using.

Variations: Add 1 tsp sliced onion...add 1 tsp fresh or 1/4 tsp dried rosemary and/or oregano.

Fake Mayonnaise

2 tbsp soy flour	oil (optional)
3 tbsp vinegar	1/2 tsp salt
3 tbsp water	onion to taste
3 tbsp parsley	1/4 tsp basil

Brown the flour in a dry pan; cool. Blend the flour and water. Using a double boiler, heat this mixture, then slowly beat in the oil. Add the salt and vinegar, then the other seasonings. Note: this dressing is not recommended for daily use due to its high fat content.

Tofu Mayonnaise

6 oz tofu, drained and pressed	1/2 tsp salt
1 tbsp oil	2 tbsp vinegar

Combine all ingredients in a blender and puree until smooth. Put the mayonnaise in a covered container and refrigerate. Do not store more than 3 days (or freeze instead).

Cole Slaw Dressing

1/2 cup sugar   1/3 cup oil
1 tsp salt   3/4 cup vinegar

See Phase 4 Cole Slaw recipe for serving directions.

Tofu Dip

6-8 oz firm tofu   1 cup fresh spinach
salt to taste   1/8 tsp oregano
                                  1/2 tsp basil

Rinse tofu and dry. Steam the spinach until tender (8-12 mins). Blend all the ingredients with just enough water to blend (about 2 tbsps). Blend at high speed for a few seconds, then stir by hand; repeat this process until the mayonnaise is smooth. Serve as a dip for raw or cooked vegetables.

Variations: Substitute your favorite steamed vegetable for the spinach...to use as a salad dressing, add 1/4-1/2 cup oil...use the mixture as a spread for rice cakes...add 1-2 tbsp oil to the dip and heat this mixture to use it as a sauce for steamed vegetables or rice noodles.

5.5 Rice Dishes

Ground or whole toasted sesame, sunflower, or pumpkin seeds may be stirred into cooked rice for variety. The flavor of cooked rice can also be changed with a dash of soy sauce (tangy and salty) or vanilla (sweet), or with a bit of minced dill. Let your taste buds decide what Phase 3 flavorings you might like to try adding to your staple, rice.

P3 Rice and Carrots

Follow the Phase 1 and 2 recipes (p. 65), adding cooked vegetables from Phase 3. Stir them into the rice when it has finished cooking.

Sushi Rice

2 1/2 cups short-grain rice   2 1/2 cups cold water
3 tbsp sugar   2 1/2 tsp salt
                                  4 tbsp vinegar

Wash rice several times. Drain the rice for 30 mins, then put it in saucepan with the water. Bring the water to a boil, cover the pan, turn the heat to low, and cook for 15 mins. Remove from heat, let stand, covered, for 10 mins. Mix the remaining ingredients, stirring well to dissolve the sugar. Pour this mixture over the rice, mix gently, and cool to room temperature. Serve with steamed safe vegetables.

Spiced Rice

2 tsp olive oil
2 tbsp minced onion
1 cup uncooked rice

2 cups chicken stock
1 tsp marjoram (or more to taste)

Heat the oil in a heavy medium saucepan over low heat. Saute the onion, then add the rice and saute for 1 min, stirring constantly. Add the stock and marjoram. Bring to a boil over moderate heat. Lower the heat and cover the pan. Simmer 18-20 mins, until all the stock is absorbed. Remove from the heat. Fluff with a fork, then recover and let stand 5 mins longer.

Ketan

2 cups glutinous (sweet/sticky) rice

3 cups water
1 tsp vanilla
brown sugar

Wash the rice. Put the rice and water in a large saucepan. Bring to a boil, then reduce the heat and cover. Cook for about 1 hour. This rice will be quite sticky. Drizzle with vanilla and stir. Melt the brown sugar. To serve the ketan, sprinkle with Klapper (see p. 124) and drizzle with melted sugar. Best when warm.

5.6 Soups, Stocks, and Appetizers

P3 Split Pea Soup

2 cups dried green split peas
4 cups chicken stock
6 cups water
2 tsp tamari wheat-free soy sauce (optional)

1/2 tbsp olive oil (optional)
1 large onion, chopped (1 cup)
1/4 tsp black pepper
1 cup chopped carrots
1 cup chopped celery

In a heavy, large saucepan, bring the peas and water to a boil, and boil for 2 mins. Turn off the heat and let stand for 1 hr. Saute the onion, carrots, and celery in a non-stick pan (or heat the oil if necessary), stirring, for about 5 mins. Add the vegetables to the peas. Add the 4 cups of stock, tamari, and pepper. Bring to a boil, then simmer, partially covered, for about 1 1/2 hrs (check occasionally and add water if necessary). Serve as is or puree the soup in a blender or food processor and reheat it. If desired, the soup can be thinned with water or extra stock.

Tofu-Spinach Soup

150g tofu

125g spinach

2 green onions

8 dL safe chicken stock

safe oil

Cut the spinach in thin strips and cut these in 1 1/2 cm pieces. Finely chop the green onions. Cut the tofu into 1 1/2 cm cubes. Heat a small amount of oil in a wok and stir-fry 1 tbsp of green onion. Add the stock and bring to a boil. Add the tofu and spinach and bring to a boil again. Season with salt and pepper to taste. Serve garnished with the remaining green onion.

Variations: Substitute lettuce for the spinach...garnish with parsley.

Creamy Carrot Soup

10 carrots

1/2 cup soy milk powder

1 tbsp oil (optional)

1 cup water

7 cups stock

salt

1 tbsp rice flour

2 tsp thyme

Dice the carrots into small pieces and saute them with the thyme for 5 mins, using a non-stick saucepan (or the oil if necessary). Add the stock, cooking this until the carrots are soft. Add the seasonings. Liquify the mixture in a blender, then return it to the stove. Blend the water, thickener, and soy milk powder together until it is smooth. Add this to the soup, stirring constantly. Simmer gently for 30 mins.

Basic Tofu Stock

4 oz tofu

1/2 small onion, chopped

1/2 cup chopped celery

3/4 cup chopped carrot

4 1/2 cups cold water

Phase 3

Combine all the ingredients in a large pot. Bring to a boil, then simmer for 45 mins. Strain the stock. This stock can be refrigerated up to 5 days or frozen up to 2 months. Use this stock as a substitute for meat/poultry stock.

Appetizers

Celery Flowers
Mix tofu, orange squash (to add color), rice flour and a safe herb. Try to achieve the consistency of cream cheese. Wash all the celery sticks from one head of celery. Keep them lined up in the order that you take them apart. Pat dry. Spread the filling into all the sticks and, starting with the center sticks, put them together with the filling facing towards the inside. When all the pieces are back together, tie the head at the top and bottom with string. Wrap the celery in wax paper or Saran wrap and place it in the fridge until set, preferably overnight. When ready to serve, slice it into 1/2" pieces.

5.7 Entrees

P3 Turkey/Chicken Patties
Follow Phase 1 and 2 recipes, adding finely diced fresh dill to the meat mixture.

P3 Chicken Pangang
Follow the Phase 2 recipe (p. 69) and add 4 tbsp soy sauce and 1/2 tsp lemon juice or vinegar to the onion mixture.

Chicken/Turkey Casserole

2 - 10oz pkgs frozen broccoli	1 lb cooked chicken or turkey
1/2 cup sesame seeds	4 tbsp rice flour
2 cups Chicken/Turkey Stock	1 cup cooked rice

Mix the rice flour with the stock, cooking over medium heat until thickened and smooth. Season this gravy to taste with safe herbs. Stir in the rice. Put the broccoli in a casserole dish and put the chicken/turkey on top. Cover with the rice mixture and sprinkle with sesame seeds (mix the seeds with a little oil if desired). Bake, uncovered, 20-25 mins until brown.

Marinated Fish

Arrange leftover cold broiled fish fillets in a single layer in a baking dish. Top with sliced onion if desired. Cover with a vinaigrette dressing (see p. 98). Sprinkle with your choice of basil, dill, and/or thyme, and season with salt and/or pepper. Cover with plastic wrap or foil, and refrigerate 24 hours or overnight. Serve with a green or rice salad.

Lemon Butter Cod

3 lbs cod fillets
lemon juice
1 cup milk-free margarine

6-8 rice crackers
1 cup rice flour
parsley flakes

Rinse cod fillets under cold water. Cut them into 3-4" pieces. Crush the crackers and mix thoroughly with the flour. Roll the fish pieces in this mixture until they are well-coated. Deep-fry the fish in hot oil until coating is crispy (not more than 5 mins). Keep the fish in the oven so it remains warm. Melt the margarine and add a small amount of lemon juice and parsley to taste. Serve the fish on a bed of rice with the lemon butter sauce drizzled over top.

Fish Pangang

500g cod
4 tbsp soy sauce

2 tbsp vinegar
salt to taste
pepper to taste

Sprinkle the cod fillets with salt and pepper. Place the fillets in a casserole dish. Mix the soy sauce and vinegar and pour this over the fillets. Broil the fish for 10-15 mins, until cooked.

Variations: Add 1 tbsp sugar to the soy mixture and marinate the fish in this mixture for about 2 hours prior to grilling...add 1 chopped onion and 3 tbsp water to the mixture...serve with a sauce of 1 tbsp soy sauce, 2 tbsp water, 1 tbsp vinegar or lemon juice, and salt and pepper to taste.

P3 Meatballs

Follow the Phase 2 recipe (see p. 73) and mix in 1/2 tbsp minced dill...1 tbsp ketchup...2 tbsp soy sauce...1/2 tsp mustard...1 tbsp coconut, 1 tbsp brown sugar, and 1/2 tbsp lemon juice.

Braised Short Ribs

3 lbs beef short ribs
1 onion, sliced
1/4 tsp thyme
1 tbsp vinegar

2 tbsp ketchup
1/2 cup water
dash of salt
dash of pepper

Cut the ribs into serving-sized pieces. Place them in a tinfoil-lined casserole and dredge with salt and pepper. Mix the remaining ingredients in a bowl. When well-blended, pour over the meat. Cover and bake at 300F for 2-3 hrs (until tender).

P3 Roast Lamb
Follow the Phase 2 recipe (p. 74), adding 1 bay leaf along with the onion to make the gravy...sprinkle the roast with Dill-Rosemary Salt (p. 122).

Glazed Lamb Chops
4 lamb chops	1/4 cup honey
1/4 cup mustard	dash salt
	dash pepper

Heat the mustard, honey, salt, and pepper over low heat, stirring occasionally. Keep the sauce warm. Follow the recipe for Broiled Lamb Chops on p. 74 and brush the chops with the mustard mixture before and after turning them. Pour the remaining sauce over the chops and serve.

Tofu, made from soybeans, is a good complementary protein source. It is an excellent source of essential amino acids and is also rich in vitamins and minerals.

Fried Tofu
Tofu can be scrambled and fried like eggs. Cook well and season. You may stir-fry vegetables along with the tofu. You may also finish the cooking by adding a water/tamari (wheat-free soy sauce) mixture to the pan, stirring the tofu in it, and letting the mixture simmer, covered, for a few minutes.

Deep-fried Tofu
12 oz firm tofu, pressed
oil
1/2 tsp salt

Cut the tofu crosswise into pieces about the size of French fries. Heat sufficient oil in a wok, skillet, or deep-fryer. Deep-fry the tofu until golden brown. Drain and pat off exces oil, then sprinkle with salt. Serve hot.

5.7.1 Grilling

Grilled and BBQ foods may be considered treats for parties and special occassions. Regular cooking over open flames may not be a healthy practice, however, and is not recommended for routine meals. The main objections are the chemicals in smoke and carcinogens which develop in burned tissues. Some of the food preparation ideas can safely be applied to regular and convection oven cooking or electric rotissaries.

Oven and outdoor grilling techniques can be used for a wide variety of foods making easy buffet-style meals. You can grill whole poultry or fish, poultry pieces, beef or lamb cuts, fish fillets, or shish kebabs (cubes of poultry, fish, beef, lamb, tofu, vegetables, and/or fruit).

Grilling Tips

1. Preheat the barbecue or oven before grilling any food. Some outdoor grills may take 40 mins or longer to heat up to the correct temperature. Outdoors, use a propane barbecue or use charcoal or mesquite in eg. a hibachi. When the coals are white, you can begin barbecuing.

2. To save time cook chicken or beef partially prior to grilling it; grill for the last 15-20 mins of cooking time. Use the microwave for either or simmer chicken pieces or beef ribs in a stock pot.

3. If you are grilling delicate foods or unskewered small pieces, place them in a wire grill basket or on a piece of tinfoil so they do not break apart or fall through the grill. Using tinfoil makes for easier cleanup as well.

4. If you are using a marinade, mix it up in a large plastic bag and add the foods you are marinating to this. Seal the bag tightly and place it in a pan in the refrigerator. Using a bag makes it easier to turn foods to ensure even marinading and makes clean-up simple.

5. If you use metal skewers for shish kebabs, be careful removing them from the grill and serving them as they will be hot. If you use bamboo skewers, soak them in water for 1/2 hr prior to use so they will not burn.

Rubs are mixtures of ground seasonings which are rubbed on the surface of the food prior to grilling; they produce a flavorful, crispy skin. Marinades are seasoned liquids to flavor and tenderize food to be grilled. Barbecue sauces may be used for basting foods while grilling or for dipping afterwards.

Basic Rub
Mix 1 tbsp oil (more or less depending on the size of pieces) with salt and pepper to taste. Rub this mixture on the poultry.

Variation: Add 1/8 tsp or more of safe ground dried herbs of your choice to the rub.

Basic Juice Marinade
Use the juice from canned peaches/pears as sweet poultry marinade.

Variation: Add 1/8 tsp or more of safe ground dried herbs of your choice and/or pepper to the marinade.

Basic Barbecue Sauce
Make Pear Juice Gravy (see p. 40) and add salt, pepper, and/or safe ground dried herbs to taste.

Shish Kebabs
Skewer your choices of:
- chicken or turkey cubes, precooked
- zucchini cubes
- broccoli cubes, steamed for 5 mins
- cubed canned peaches
- cauliflower cubes, steamed for 5 mins
- onion chunks
- cubed apples
- cubed cantaloupe or honeydew melon
- peaches, cubed or sliced
- pears, cubed or sliced
- plum slices

Place foods alternately on the skewers until each skewer is filled. To broil in the oven, place the skewers on a foil-lined pan with 2 cups of water on it. Brush each skewer with a mixture of oil, salt, and safe herbs. Broil 5-12 mins, until tender and browned. To barbecue, place a piece of foil on the grill and place the skewers on top. Brush each skewer with the oil/salt/safe herbs mixture. Close the barbecue lid and cook until tender and browned. Serve immediately.

P3 Shish Kebabs

Chicken Setan

1 minced onion	4 tbsp soy sauce
1 tsp safe oil	salt to taste
2 1/2 dL water	1 tbsp brown sugar
	1 Kg chicken breasts

Remove the chicken bones, skin, and fat; set the chicken aside. Grind the onion and salt together. Heat the oil (or use a nonstick pan) and fry the onion mixture for 2 mins. Add the water, soy sauce, and sugar. Bring to a boil and let it boil for 3 mins. Add the chicken pieces, stir, reduce the heat and simmer 45 mins or until the chicken is done. Take the chicken out of the pan and put it on the grill until it is browned (or place the chicken in an ovenproof pan and grill in a preheated oven). Serve over rice, using the onion-water as a sauce.

Barbecued Chicken Breasts

3-4 lbs chicken breasts	1/2 cup fresh or 2 tbsp dried
1 tbsp olive oil	oregano
1/4 cup fresh or 1 tbsp dried	pepper
thyme	salt

Debone the chicken and remove the skin and excess fat. Boil the chicken until it turns white (about 4 mins), then drain and cool it. Prepare the herbs; chop the fresh or crush the dried, then mix the herbs. Rub the chicken all over with the oil. Stuff the herb mixture under the chicken skin. Season the chicken with salt and pepper. Wrap the chicken in foil and let stand 1 hour at room temperature or overnight in the refrigerater (remove 1 hour before cooking). Heat the barbecue. Brown the chicken, turning once. Close the lid of the barbecue, making sure the vents are open; cook for 10 mins. Open and cook until the chicken juices are clear (prick a piece of dark meat to test) (about 20 mins).

Marinated Barbecued Turkey/Chicken
Precook boneless turkey/chicken breasts in microwave or oven with skin on. Peel back the skin and marinate meat in peach juice; use the juice to brush over the meat as it browns on the grill.

Rubbed Barbecued Turkey/Chicken
Barbecue a whole turkey/chicken after rubbing a little oil all over it (mix the oil with safe herbs if desired).

Basic Barbecued Fish
whitefish fillet
safe oil
salt

Brush each side of the fillet with oil and sprinkle with salt. Grill on the barbecue or broil in a preheated oven, about 4 mins per side.

P2 Grilled Fruit
Chunks of fruit (except berries and watermelon) can be grilled. Peaches, pears, and plums are especially good in Phase 2. Place them in a wire grilling basket or on a piece of tinfoil. Brush them with melted milk-free margarine (if desired) and/or sprinkle with sugar. Grill for 3-6 mins, stirring occasionally so that each piece is thoroughly heated. Serve warm.

HINTS: Think of rolls as "sandwiches" and choose different fillings to suit your taste. Use lettuce leaves to stuff chicken or turkey, to add moisture and texture.

Use rice polish for breading poultry, fish, or meat for frying in a non-stick pan. Add safe herbs, salt, and/or pepper to the breading if desired.

Use rice flour in place of your usual thickener to make gravy from drippings.

Phase 3 introduces the use of tofu and numerous seasonings which can be used in rubs, marinades, and barbecue sauces.

Southern Rub

2 tbsp olive oil	1 tsp dried rosemary
2 tbsp milk-free margarine	1 tsp dried thyme
1 tsp dried oregano	1 tsp onion powder
	1/2 tsp pepper

Combine all the ingredients and rub on chicken or fish.

Chicken Vinegar Marinade

1 tsp lime juice	4 tbsp olive oil
4 tbsp vinegar	2 tbsp chopped onion

Mix the ingredients and add the chicken. Cover and refrigerate overnight. Marinates 2 chicken breasts (whole or cubed).

Variations: Add salt and/or pepper to taste.

Oriental Fish Marinade

4 tbsp olive oil	1/4 cup vinegar
2 tbsp soy sauce	pepper to taste
2 tsp chopped ginger	

Combine all the ingredients and marinate the fish.

Beef Vinegar Marinade

2 tbsp olive oil	1/2 tsp salt
1 tbsp vinegar	1/2 tsp pepper

Combine all the ingredients and add 1 lb cubed beef. Marinate for 1/2 hour. When grilling, brush the beef with the marinade.

Beef Soy Marinade

1/2 tbsp fresh ginger	1 tbsp sugar
3 tbsp soy sauce	2 tbsp safe oil

Mix the ingredients and marinate beef cubes for 4 hours prior to making Shish Kebabs.

Lamb Marinade

1/3 cup vinegar	1 bay leaf
1/3 cup safe oil	dash of pepper
2 tbsp soy sauce	2 tsp dried rosemary

Combine all the ingredients and marinate 2 lbs of cubed lamb overnight in the refrigerator.

5.7.2 Gravies and Sauces

Rice Flour Gravy #2

2 tbsp rice flour	1 1/4 cup ProSobee
3 tbsp pan juices	salt

Heat the juices in a skillet. Add the rice flour and brown, stirring. Slowly add the ProSobee, stirring constantly to avoid lumps. Cook over low heat until thick and smooth, stirring often. Salt to taste.

P3 Peanut Butter Sauce

1/2 cup peanut butter	1 cup water

Mix the peanut butter with the water in a saucepan over low heat. If the sauce is too thick, add a little more water; if it is too thin, add more peanut butter. Serve warm or cold.

Phase 3

Variations: Try one or more of these variations at a time...a dash soy sauce...fry 1/2 minced onion, then add the peanut butter and water to this pan...add 1 tbsp brown sugar...use stock instead of water...use the water from cooked vegetables...add salt to taste...add a dash of vinegar or lemon juice.

Dipping Sauce #1

1/2 cup warm water	dash salt
2 tbsp soy sauce	dash pepper
	crushed peanuts

Combine ingredients and dip salad rolls in the sauce or pour a small amount of the sauce over each roll.

Dipping Sauce #2

1/4 cup water	2 tsp soy sauce
1 tbsp ketchup	1 tsp sugar
	2 tbsp crushed peanuts

In a small saucepan, combine all the ingredients. Stir over low heat for 5-10 mins until the sauce is smooth and thickened.

Variations: Use brown sugar or honey instead of white sugar...place 1 tsp of the sauce inside a lettuce wrap when adding the filling (see p. 75).

Soy Sauce with Coconut

2 tbsp flaked coconut	3 tbsp soy sauce
2 tbsp vinegar	1 tbsp brown sugar
	salt to taste

Toast the coconut over low heat in a nonstick frying pan. Grind the coconut and add it to the other ingredients. Mix well and let stand in a cool place for 1 hour before use.

5.8 Baking

Baking in Phase 3 includes the use of soy milk and/or infant soy formula as a liquid. Soy milk is the consistency of cow's milk, while infant soy formula can be substituted for evaporated milk or diluted with water to replace cow's milk. Tofu can also be used now, as in pie or tart fillings. Pumpkin, sunflower, and sesame seeds can be added to a variety of baked products for flavor and decoration. Coconut is another flavor addition that is especially good for cakes and cookies. Vanilla is often considered a baking staple for flavoring. Carob can be used as a chocolate substitute in baking.

5.8.1 Substitutions

Wheat Flour Substitutions

1 tbsp wheat flour =   1/2 tbsp rice flour/starch *or*
      1/2 tbsp arrowroot starch *or*
      1/2 tbsp Tapioca starch *or*
      2 tsp tapioca/tapioca flour *or*
      1/2 cup cooked rice *or*
      2 tbsp uncooked rice

Egg Substitutions
Pureed baby food/fruit can be used as a binder in place of egg (it will also sweeten the final product). Use leftover *sticky rice* to bind rice pancakes. Gelatin (Phase 4) may be tried as a binder in breads, especially those made with rice flour. Soften the gelatin in half the liquid called for in the recipe, then heat this mixture just enough to dissolve the gelatin. Add this to the remaining liquid. 1 cup *rice puffs* to 1 lb ground meat binds meat loaf or hamburgers.

1 egg =   1 tsp baking soda + 2 tbsp vinegar *or*
      2 tbsp baking powder + 1 tsp vinegar *or*
      1 tsp soy lecithin

Pasta Substitutions
Use *wheat-free pasta*, eg. rice noodles (made of rice and water in Phase 1, or rice flour and water in Phase 2) or *100% buckwheat noodles* (Phase 4), or *spaghetti squash* (Phase 1).

Chocolate Substitutions
Chocolate = carob powder or chips

Dairy Substitutions
Try *fruit juice* (eg. apple or pear juice) instead of dairy products in baked goods. If the recipe calls for yeast or baking powder, work very quickly as fruit juice/puree tends to neutralize their rising action.

Instead of milk/cream in sauces, try *water, stock, or fruit juice*.

Milk = equal parts undiluted infant soy formula and water (eg. a ready-to-use infant soy formula; i-Soyalac, ProSobee, Nursoy).

Evaporated milk = undiluted infant soy formula (eg.ProSobee Concentrated Liquid)

Ice cream = soya or tofu based "non-dairy" ice creams are available as well as rice-based frozen desserts. Sherbets, based on fruit, sugar, and gelatin are also worth trying.

1 Cup *sour cream* in a recipe = 4 tbsp safe starch stirred into 1 cup water + 1 cup vinegar. Tofu can often be substituted for custard.

Some of the recipes call for safe *shortening/margarine*. In general, the use of such shortenings is not recommended. Relatively safe substitutes for butter, regular shortening, and regular margarine are milk-free margarines, colored with beta carotene, or soy lecithin spreads. However, you will encounter fewer problems by using vegetable oil as a substitute for shortening and margarine. Never melt margarine for cooking applications - always use a vegetable oil.

5.8.2 Biscuits and Dumplings

Rice Flour Biscuits

1 cup rice flour	1/2 cup ProSobee liquid
2 tbsp oil	1 tbsp baking powder
1/4 tsp salt	1/2 cup water

Preheat the oven to 400F. Combine the dry ingredients in a large bowl. Add oil, then stir in ProSobee and water, mixing well. Lightly knead the dough 10 times on a lightly floured surface. Make biscuits and bake them on an oiled cookie sheet until golden brown (15-20 mins).

Basic Filled Dumplings

2 drops oil
1/2 cup celery
2 tbsp soy sauce
1/2 cup onions

2 tbsp green onions
2 tsp safe oil (if needed)
2 cups ground chicken/turkey
pepper to taste
salt to taste

Dough:
3 cups rice flour
boiling water

Mince the onions, green onion, and celery. Heat a non-stick skillet (or use the safe oil). Add the onions, celery, chicken, and salt to taste, stirring until the chicken turns white. Turn the heat off. Add the soy sauce, 2 drops of oil, pepper, and green onions. Mix well and remove the mixture to a bowl; set aside. In a bowl, add the boiling water gradually to the rice flour, stirring constantly until the dough resembles pie dough (ie. thick). Cover the bowl for 10 mins so the heat will cook the dough. Knead until smooth. Divide the dough into golf-ball size pieces. Roll each piece out with a well-oiled rolling pin into a very thin round. Make a pouch in each round, folding one part up so it rests halfway up the remainder of the dough. Fill the pouch with a heaping tbsp of filling. Fold the top half of the dough down and seal the pouch by pinching the edges with firmly. Place the dumplings on a heatproof dish which will fit into a steamer and steam for 15 mins. Serve hot or cold. Note: If the dough falls apart while rolling it out or while making the pouch, this means it was not cooked long enough, or the boiling water was added too slowly and the bowl was too cold; steam the dough for 5 mins and roll/pouch it again.

5.8.3 Cakes and Cupcakes

Wacky Cake

1 1/2 cups rice flour
1 cup sugar
1 tsp baking soda
1/4 tsp salt

1/3 cup oil
1 tbsp white vinegar
1/2 tsp vanilla
3/4 cup cold water

Topping:
1/3 cup milk-free margarine
1 cup sugar
1/4 tsp vanilla

Preheat oven to 350F. Sift dry ingredients together. Put into 8" square pan. Make 3 wells; pour oil into large well, vinegar into medium well, and vanilla into small well. Pour water all over and stir with fork until dissolved. Bake 30-40 mins (test with a toothpick - if it comes out clean, cake is done). Remove cake. Preheat broiler and put rack 6" from broiler. Spread topping on warm cake and broil 2-3 mins until golden.

Rice Cake

1 cup rice flour	1 tbsp oil
1/4 tsp salt	1/3 cup sugar
1 tbsp baking powder	1/2 cup - 2 tbsp water
	1 tsp vanilla

Preheat the oven to 350F. Sift together the dry ingredients, then add the water, oil, and vanilla. Beat for 1 min. Oil a small (13"x6"x2") pan and pour in the batter. Bake for 15 mins, then reduce the heat to 325F and bake 45 mins.

<u>Variations</u>: Add blueberries or carob chips to the batter for extra flavor...make cupcakes by oiling muffin tins instead of a pan. Baking time is less, so watch them carefully.

Rice Flour Cupcakes

2/3 cup hot water	3 tsp baking powder
1/4 tsp salt	2 tsp oil
1 1/2 cups rice flour	1 tsp vanilla
	1/4 cup sugar

Preheat the oven to 400F. Divide the flour in half. Pour hot water over one half. Cream the sugar and oil/safe shortening and beat this into the flour mixture. Add the remaining ingredients, mixing well. Bake in oiled muffin tins for 20 mins.

5.8.4 Frostings

Caramelized Frosting

2 cups brown sugar	2/3 cup water
1 tsp vanilla	3 tbsp oil

Combine the sugar and water in a saucepan. Stir slowly while bringing to a rapid boil; stir constantly until the mixture reachs the soft ball stage. Remove from the heat, add the oil and vanilla, and let stand until lukewarm. Then beat the frosting until it is thick and no longer shiny. Spread this quickly over the cake.

Carob Frosting

1/3 cup carob powder
1 tbsp vanilla

1/4 cup honey
1 tbsp oil
1/4 cup water

Mix all the ingredients in a blender. Or put all the ingredients in a saucepan, increasing the water to 1/2 cup and adding 1 tbsp safe thickener (eg. arrowroot), and heat the mixture in a until it thickens. Spread this over warm cake.

Creamy Icing

1 tbsp milk-free margarine
1/4 cup water or safe juice

1 tsp vanilla
2 1/2 cups icing sugar

Soften the margarine, then add the vanilla and water. Add half the icing sugar and mix. Continue adding icing sugar until a smooth, thick consistency is achieved.

Vanilla Glaze

1/3 cup milk-free margarine
2 cups icing sugar

1 1/2 tsp vanilla
2-4 tbsp water

Melt the margarine in a saucepan then stir in the vanilla and sugar. Add the water gradually, until the desired consistency is achieved.

5.8.5 Cookies

P3 Shortbread

1 1/2 cups rice flour
1/2 cup milk-free margarine

2 tbsp sugar
1/4 tsp salt
2 tbsp prepared ProSobee

Preheat oven to 350F. Stir 1 cup rice flour and the other dry ingredients into the shortening. Add the ProSobee. Knead the dough, gradually adding the remaining 1/2 cup rice flour. When the dough is cracking, shape it into 2 or 3 balls. Press the balls into rounds on an ungreased cookie sheet. Press around the outer edge of each round with a fork and prick each round several times. Bake 15-25 mins. When cool, store in an airtight cookie tin.

Variation: Add 3/4 cup of toasted sunflower seeds to the dough.

Crispy Rice Cookies

1 cup brown sugar
1 cup rice flour
1/2 tsp vanilla
1/4 tsp salt
1/4 cup apple juice

3/4 tsp baking soda
1/4 cup melted milk-free margarine
1/4 tsp baking powder
2 cups Rice Krispies

Preheat the oven to 350F. Blend the sugar, vanilla, apple juice, and melted shortening well. Add the sifted dry ingredients, then the Rice Krispies. Shape the dough into small balls and flatten them on a well-oiled cookie sheet. Bake 10 mins. Let stand 2-3 mins before removing them as they crumble easily. Cool thoroughly on racks.

Rice Flour Cookies

3 tbsp milk-free margarine
1/2 tsp salt
2 tbsp brown sugar

3 tsp baking powder
1 tsp vanilla
about 1 cup water
2 cups rice flour

Preheat the oven to 325F. Cream the shortening and sugar. Add the vanilla. Sift together the remaining dry ingredient and stir them into the shortening mixture alternately with water. Add just enough water to make a thick dough. Roll the dough out thinly on a lightly floured surface. Cut the cookies. Place them on an oiled cookie sheet. Bake until lightly browned, about 10 mins.

Sesame Cookies

1 cup milk-free margarine
2 cups rice flour
sesame seeds
1/2 tsp salt

1 tsp vanilla
1/4 cup sugar
strawberry/raspberry preserves/jam

Cream the margarine and sugar together; blend in the vanilla extract and salt. Add the flour; mix well. Shape tbsps (or tsps) of dough into balls; roll these in sesame seeds. Place them on ungreased cookie sheets; flatten slightly. Indent the center of each; fill with preserves/jam. Bake at 400F 10-12 mins.

Carob Cookies

2 cups sugar
6 tbsp carob powder
1/2 cup milk-free margarine

pinch of salt
1/2 cup water
1 tsp vanilla
4 cups puffed rice

Combine the sugar, margarine, water, carob, and salt in a saucepan and bring to a rolling boil. Remove from the stove and add the vanilla and puffed rice. Mix well. Drop by tablespoons onto waxed paper. Cool.

Nut Butter Balls

1 cup soft milk-free margarine
1/4-1/2 cup sugar or icing sugar
1/2 tsp salt

2 tsp vanilla
2 cups sifted rice flour
1-2 cups finely chopped peanuts

Cream margarine and sugar together. Add salt, vanilla, flour, and nuts; mix well. Chill dough until it is easy to handle. Preheat oven to 350F. Roll the dough into small balls. Bake for 12-15 mins. After baking, roll in sugar. Makes 4-5 dozen.

5.8.6 Pies and Crackers

P3 Soy Milk Pie Crust

1 1/2 cups rice flour
1/4 cup soy milk

1/2 tsp salt
1 cup oil

Combine the dry ingredients in a large bowl and the liquid in a smaller bowl. Add the liquid to dry. Press the dough into a pie plate. Add your choice of pie filling. Bake the pie at 400F for 15 mins, then reduce the heat to 350F and bake for 30 mins or until filling is cooked.

Variation: Increase the dough mixture and crumble leftovers over the top of the pie.

Soy Milk Pastry

2 cups rice flour
2/3 cup oil

1 1/4 tsp salt

3 tbsp soy milk or ProSobee
Ready-to-Use

1 tsp herbs or 1-2 tbsp seeds
(optional)

Preheat oven to 450F. Mix dry ingredients in a large bowl. In another bowl, mix liquid ingredients until creamy. Add liquid to a well in the dry ingredients, stirring with a fork until mixed. If dough is too sticky, add a little more flour. Form into two balls. Pat into pie plates or tart tins or roll out the dough between two pieces of wax paper, remove one piece, place dough into pie pan and remove the other piece (this is the more difficult method). This pastry must be thicker than wheat flour pastry. Prick the dough all over with a fork. Bake for 10-12 mins or until lightly browned. Watch the dough as it cooks, so you can release any air bubbles that appear. The pastry must be cooked before it is filled and the filling cannot be cooked in the shell. Makes 2 - 8" crusts or 5-6 tarts.

Vanilla Pie Crust

3/4 cup sifted rice flour
1/4 cup milk-free margarine
1 tsp sugar

1/3 cup warm water
1/2 tsp salt
1/2 tsp vanilla

Blend the rice flour, sugar, salt, and shortening. Add the water and vanilla, blending into a soft dough. Refrigerate for 15 mins. Sprinkle a piece of wax paper and a rolling pin with rice flour. Carefully roll the dough onto the wax paper. Place a second piece of floured wax paper on top of the dough. Roll the wax-papered dough back onto the rolling pin. Remove the outer piece of wax paper and unroll the dough into the pie plate. Remove the other piece of wax paper. Use a fork to prick the sides and bottom of the dough. Steam the crust to prevent cracking by inverting an empty pie plate in a large pot containing with 1/2" water. When the water is boiling, put the crust-containing pie plate onto the inverted one. Cover and steam for 15 mins. Then bake the crust for 20 mins at 350F. When cool, fill with pie filling.

5.8.7 Pie Fillings

Strawberry Tofu Puree
See p. 123.

Chicken Filling

4 oz chicken/turkey, cooked
and diced
1-3 tsp water or vegetable juice

4 oz soft tofu
1/2 safe herb

| 1 1/2 tbsp grated raw/cooked vegetable | 1 tsp salt |
| | Soy Milk Pastry (see p. 118) |

Place all filling ingredients into a pot and cook, stirring occasionally. If filling needs thickening, add 1-3 tsp rice flour and cook a little longer. Cool and pour into 4-5 precooked tart shells (you may wish to make pastry lids as well).

5.9 Treats, Desserts, and Drinks

5.9.1 Spreads and Seasonings

Spreads made from cooked dried beans, tofu, nuts, or seeds are high in protein. Use nut and seed butters sparingly as they are high in fats. Natural-style peanut butter without sugar, salt, or additives can be tried at this time.

P3 Peanut Butter
250 g shelled roasted peanuts
1 tbsp safflower oil

Blend the oil and peanuts together until smooth. Refrigerate.

Sunflower Butter
Puree 1 cup sunflower seeds (shelled) , 6 tbsp oil, and salted to taste in a blender to desired consistency.

Sesame Butter
Grind raw or roasted sesame seeds, then add oil or water until the butter achieves the desired consistency.

Strawberry Jam
Prepare the jars as instructed in the Apple Jelly recipe (p.81). Crush 8 cups washed strawberries. Mix the berries with 5 cups sugar and 2 tbsp lemon juice in a Dutch oven. Boil over high heat, stirring frequently. When the jam is thick and translucent (about 25 mins), skim the foam off and immediately pour the jam into the sterilized jars, filling to within 1/4" of top. Seal as per Apple Jelly.

Variations: Substitute 8 cups of peeled, diced peaches or 8 cups crushed raspberries for the strawberries.

Tahini

1/4 cup finely ground sesame seeds	2 tbsp water
	1 tsp lemon juice
	1/2 tsp oil

Combine all ingredients in a blender.

Variation: Mix the tahini with toasted sesame seeds and honey.

Tofu Spread

Mash tofu and mix it with chopped green onion, fresh minced dill, lemon juice, and pepper.

Variation: Add sweet or savory flavorings of your choice to mashed tofu.

Bean Spread

Mash cooked lima beans and flavor them with chopped green onion, vinegar, and a dash of ketchup.

Zesty Avocado Spread

1-2 ripe avocados	vinegar
onion juice	finely chopped onion
	salt

Peel, pit, and mash the avocados. Add vinegar and salt to taste. Add the onion and/or onion juice to taste if desired. Serve on rice crackers or use as a dip.

Roasted Seeds

Roast sunflower, pumpkin, or sesame seeds by either of these methods.

Frying Pan Method: A small amount of oil may be used. Put seeds in a frying pan over medium heat. Season with salt if desired. Stir the seeds fairly frequently to ensure even roasting. Turn down the heat if the seeds begin to brown or burn before they are completely dry.

Oven Method: Put the seeds on a cookie sheet (toss the seeds in a small amount of oil first if desired). Roast them at 350F for 15-20 mins, stirring every 5 mins to ensure even roasting. Cool the seeds prior to eating as they will not be totally crunchy when first removed from the oven.

Sesame Seasoning

1 cup sesame seeds
1 tsp salt

Preheat the oven to 325F. Salt the sesame seeds, then toast them until they are light brown (about 10 mins), stirring often to avoid burning. Cool, then grind the seeds.

Dill-Rosemary Salt

2 tsp dried dill will	1 tsp salt
1/2 tsp dried rosemary	1/4 tsp pepper

Mix together.

5.9.2 Snacks and Desserts

Although peanuts and seeds are introduced in Phase 3, it is best to use them as additions to salads and cooking, rather than as snack foods. Over-consumption can lead to compulsive eating and cravings.

P3 Granola
Choose of any or all of the following:

hulled sunflower seeds	puffed rice
pumpkin seeds	flaked coconut
sesame seeds	chopped dates

Roast the sunflower seeds (if using) in a heavy frying pan over medium heat, stirring frequently. After 5-10 mins, add your choice of pumpkin seeds and/or puffed rice and roast for a couple of mins. Add sesame seeds, dates, and coconut just before removing the frying pan from the stove.

P3 Fruit Salad
Choose any combination of fruits mentioned on p. 3.6.3 and 4.10.2 and toss together with sunflower, pumpkin, or sesame seeds. Chill and serve over tofu ice cream, if desired.

Tofu Ice Cream

18 oz tofu	3 tbsp honey
1/4 tsp vanilla	1/8 tsp salt

Chill the tofu well. Puree 12 oz of tofu, the honey, vanilla, and salt for about 1 min. Pour into a container and cover, freezing overnight. The next day, cube the frozen tofu. Puree the remaining 6 oz tofu until smooth at high speed, then gradually add the frozen tofu, pureeing until the mixture is smooth and thick. Serve immediately.

Variation: Fresh or frozen fruits may be added toward the end of the first pureeing.

Honey Ice Cream

1/4 cup oil
1 cup soy milk powder

1/2 cup honey
2 1/2 cups water
1 tbsp vanilla (optional)

Blend all the ingredients well. Pour the mixture into metal cake pans and freeze. Beat the mixture when it is partially frozen and then freeze it again to achieve a creamy texture.

Variation: Substitute fruit for the vanilla to flavor the ice cream.

Strawberry Tofu Puree

7-8 oz tofu
2 tbsp honey

2 cups fresh strawberries
1 tsp vanilla

Puree the tofu, 1 cup of strawberries, honey, and vanilla in a blender until smooth and creamy. To serve, top with the remaining strawberries.

Carob Tofu Puree: Substitute 2 tbsp carob for the 1 cup of strawberries.

Variation #2: Use these purees as pie fillings for baked pie shells. Chill prior to serving.

P3 Puffed Rice Candy

Follow the recipe on p. 85, adding 1/2 tsp vanilla with the salt and puffed rice.

Sesame Seed Candy

1 cup sesame seeds
1 tbsp honey

Grind the seeds. Add the honey, kneading until the mixture is fairly stiff. Serve as is or break it into pieces and roll in these in whole sesame seeds.

Variation: Add grated carrot just before adding the honey.

Sesame Seed Candy #2

2 cups sesame seeds
1 cup honey
2 tbsp water

Preheat oven to 425F. Spread seeds in the bottom of an 8"x12" pan. Dribble honey over the seeds. Pour in water and mix together. Bake until seeds begin to brown. Harden in the freezer before cutting.

Carob Sesame Treats

2 tbsp sesame seeds
130g coconut

2 tbsp carob powder

2 tbsp honey
1/3 cup safe juice

Lightly brown the sesame seeds in a heavy pan over medium heat. Remove from the pan and cool. Use a food processor to combine all the ingredients except for 30g of coconut. Form the mixture into small balls and roll these in the reserved coconut. Refrigerate until firm. Makes 3 dozen.

Carob Fudge
1/2 cup oil
1/2 tsp vanilla

1/2 cup honey
1 cup carob powder

Beat oil, honey, and vanilla until very smooth. Stir in carob powder. Press into lightly oiled 8"x8"x2" pan and chill to harden.

Creamy Fudge
2 cups brown sugar
1/2 tsp vanilla

2 tbsp oil
6 tbsp water

Bring the sugar, water, and oil to a boil in a saucepan, stirring constantly. Boil to soft ball stage (if you immerse the saucepan in cold water, it may form a ball more readily). Add the vanilla, beating until a lighter color is achieved. Pour the mixture into oiled pie plates; score into squares.

Whipped Cream
1/2 cup soy milk
1/2 cup oil

1 tbsp honey
1/4 tsp vanilla

Blend the soy milk and vanilla. Gradually add the oil and then the honey.

Variations: Substitute 1/4 cup safe berries for the vanilla...add 2 tsp carob powder for chocolate whipped cream.

Klapper
1/2-1 cup coconut
about 1 tbsp water
1 tsp vanilla

Add some water to the coconut to moisturize it, then stir in the vanilla. Serve over Ketan (p. 101).

Seroendeng
1 minced onion
salt
200g coconut

2 tbsp brown sugar
150g blanched peanuts

Crush the onion and salt together. Mix in the coconut. Toast in a very small amount of oil in a heavy pan until lightly browned. Remove from the heat and stir in the sugar. Let cool. Add the peanuts just before serving. Serve over rice.

5.9.3 Beverages

A cup of hot water with a touch of lemon and honey is a beverage option in Phase 3.

Some of these advanced beverage recipes call for soy milk. You may wish to try them using infant soy formula first, as this is better tolerated than regular soy milk. For 1 cup soy milk, use 1 cup ProSobee Ready-to-Use or 1/2 cup ProSobee Concentrated liquid diluted with 1/2 cup water (or to taste).

To improve the flavor of soy milk, blend one or more of the following ingredients with 1 cup of soy milk:
- 3/4 cup frozen safe berries
- 2 tbsp safe pureed fruit
- dash of salt
- 2 tsp vanilla

P3 Fruit Soy Drink
1/2 cup soy milk
1/2 cup peach and/or pear nectar

Blend the ingredients well and serve immediately.

Soy Milk Shake
1/4 cup soy milk   1/4 cup cold water
1 tbsp sugar (optional)   1/2 cup safe fruit juice
                                    1/2 cup crushed ice

Blend all the ingredients well and serve immediately.

Vanilla Soy Drink
1 cup soy milk   1/2 cup water
1/2 tsp vanilla   sugar or honey if desired
Blend all the ingredients well and serve immediately.

Hot Carob-Soy Drink
1 qt soy milk   1/2 tsp vanilla
3-4 tbsp carob powder   2 tbsp oil
1 tbsp honey

Blend all the ingredients except the oil until smooth and liquid. Gradually add the oil slowly, making sure the liquid remains smooth. Heat the liquid, but do not boil it; serve immediately.

Sesame Seed Milk/Cream
4 cups water
1/2 cup sesame seeds
1 tbsp sugar or honey

Grind the seeds in a blender. For milk, add 2 cups of water and blend thoroughly, then add the remaining water. For cream, add only 3/4 cup water. Strain if desired before serving.

Soaked Sesame Milk
1 cup sesame seeds
3 cups water

Crush the seeds if desired (this will cause a foam to appear on the milk). Soak the seeds in the water for 6-8 hours. Strain the liquid and bring it to a boil. Add safe flavors if desired.

CONVERSION TABLE

1 tbsp = 3 tsp	1/2 tsp = 2 mL
1/4 cup = 4 tbsp	1 tsp = 5 mL
1/3 cup = 5 1/3 tbsp	1 tbsp = 15 mL
1/2 cup = 8 tbsp	1/4 cup = 60 mL
1 cup = 16 tbsp	1/3 cup = 80 mL
1 fl oz = 2 tbsp	1/2 cup = 125 mL
1 pt = 2 cups	1 cup = 250 mL
1 qt = 2 pts	1 fl oz = 30 mL
1 gal = 4 qts	1 pt = 500 mL
1/8 tsp = 1/2 mL	1 qt = 1 L
1/4 tsp = 1 mL	1 gal = 4 L

Chapter 6

PHASE 4 ADVANCED FOOD CHOICES

Phase 4 is the final expansion of Core Diet foods. For many people, phase 4 recipes complete their Core Diet design as a long-term eating strategy. The emphasis is still on vegetable and fruit choices with more grain-substitutes and their flours for cooking and baking. Foods from the more allergic food groups - dairy, cereal grains, eggs - for example, have not re-appeared on our food list, but more satisfactory replacements are now in place. The recipes in this phase are more elaborate and serve as a more complete replacement of cuisines you were used to before developing your Core Diet. Snacks, desserts, and party ideas turn your Core Diet into a pleasant, rewarding experience which you can confidently share with guests for dinner.

Most of the newly-introduced Phase 4 foods can be considered optional or occassional foods, not daily staple foods. Their inclusion in menus and recipes increases taste and variety but may compromise food allergy control. All the recipes in earlier phases are useful with bonus of additional ingredients.

Generally in stage four we introduce new foods at a leisurely pace, perhaps one every three or four days, giving enough time to decide if the new food is well-tolerated. By continuing to use stable, early recipes and meal plans, you usually can tell if the new ingredient produces recurring symptoms. As always in the Core Program, if you have any symptoms from adding new foods you retreat to an earlier, better tolerated phase of the Core Program.

6.1 Food Choices

Bean Sprouts
Beets
Bok Choy
Cabbage
Chard
Corn
Kale
Kohlrabi
Leeks
Mushrooms
Parsnips
Potatoes
Pumpkin
Radishes
Tomatoes

Arrowroot
Buckwheat

Cornstarch
Millet
Soy Flour
Tapioca
Yeast

Apricots
Blackberries
Cherries
Coconut
Cranberries
Currants
Grapes
Mangoes
Nectarines
Oranges
Papaya
Pineapple

Prunes
Raisins

Salmon
Trout

Abalone
Crab
Lobster
Prawns
Scallops
Shrimp

Egg Yolk
Gelatin

Coconut Milk

Garlic
Marshmallows
Mint

6.1.1 Vegetables

Bean Sprouts may be introduced at this point.

Beets (Beta vulgaris) belong to the Chenopodiaceae Family and are, therefore, related to chard and spinach. Both the beet root and the leaves (beet greens) are edible. The root is about 90% water when cooked, but much of its solid content is carbohydrate, making twice as "starchy" as the beet greens. The greens, however, are much richer in iron, calcium, and Vitamins A and C. Choose firm, smooth beets as soft or rough beets tend to be woody. Choose clean, fresh greens, using criteria for selecting spinach.

Chinese Cabbages are members of the Mustard Family (Cruciferae), which includes the cabbage vegetables, mustards, rutabaga, and turnips. Two types are Brassica chinensis (bok-choy or Chinese mustard) and Brassica pekinensis (pe-tsai or celery cabbage). Chinese cabbages are more closely related to mustards and turnips than to the head-forming cabbages. They contain goitrogenic substances. These cabbages are very low in calories (11-24 Kcal per cup) and contain about 95% water. A 1 cup serving of cooked bok-choy provides almost as much calcium as a cup of milk and is a good source of potassium, iron and vitamin A.

Cabbage is a member of the mustard family (Cruciferae), Brassica oleracea. It contains goitrogenic substances (the effect may be offset by ample amounts of dietary iodine). Cabbage has a high water content (over 90%) and is low in calories (less than 35 Kcal per cup). It is a good source of potassium. Overcooking greatly reduces the nutritional value of cabbage and increases its unpleasant odors. Cabbage has a mild to moderate laxative effect due mainly to its fiber content. If you do not use the whole cabbage, wrap the rest tightly and refrigerate.

Chard, like beets, is Beta vulgaris, a member of the Chenopodiaceae Family. The leaves of chard (also known as Swiss Chard) are eaten as greens. Chard is high in water (91-91%) and low in calories. It is an excellent source of Vitamin A, iron, potassium, and magnesium and calcium. When cooking chard, remove very thick stems and cook these separately as they will take longer.

Corn, or maize, is a grain rich in carbohydrates and fats, but it lacks protein. It is only 8-11% protein and lacks lysine and tryptophan. Corn is also deficient in calcium and niacin. Unfortunately allergic reactions to corn are common often with significant behavioral disturbances in children.

Kale (Brassica oleracea) is a member of the Mustard Family and is most closely related to the wild cabbage. It is essentially the same as collards except it has curlier leaves. Cooked kale is 90% water and is low in calories. It has 6% protein (the highest of the cabbage vegetables), furnishing about the same amount of protein as an equivalent amount of cooked rice or corn, but at one quarter the calories. It is high in calcium (1 cup of cooked kale provides as much calcium as 5 oz of milk); its calcium level is three times that of its phosphorus level. It is a good source of iron and potassium, contains high amounts of Vitamin A, and fairly high amounts of Vitamin C. Note that frozen kale has half the Vitamin C of fresh, because the blanching process required for freezing destroys Vitamin C. Choose young, fresh kale as you would other greens. Kale is best cooked.

Kohlrabi, another Brassica oleracea vegetable, developed from the wild cabbage and the wild turnip. It is high in water and low in calories. It is a good source of potassium and Vitamin C, but because it is mostly stem, it is lower in most nutrients compared to other members of the Cruciferae Family. Compared to a potato, however, it has a similar protein content (2%), half the calories, and over three times the Vitamin C. Avoid kohlrabi with stems over 3" in diameter. Kohlrabi may be eaten raw, steamed, or boiled. It may also be stuffed and baked or served with a creamy sauce.

Leeks (Allium porrum) is similar to the onion. However, rather than eating the bulb, the stem and leaves are consumed. Leeks are high in water (85%) and fairly low in calories (52 Kcal per 100g). They are a good source of potassium and iron. They also are a fair source of Vitamin C. Choose leeks with dark green leaves and white stems. Wash them well, then use them raw or cooked.

Mushrooms are either Basidiomycetes (club fungi) or Ascomycetes (cup fungi, eg. truffles). Types of mushrooms include: the common cultivated type (Agaricus bisporus), oyster (Pleurotus ostreatus), padi straw (Volvariella volvaceae), shiitake (Lentinus edodes), and truffles (Tuber melanosporum; Tuber magnatum). Mushrooms are high in water (90%) and low in calories (28-35 Kcal/100 g). They contain about 20% more protein than potatoes, but less than half the calories. They are very low in calcium, vitamin A, and vitamin C, moderately low in thiamin and riboflavin, and are good sources of phosphorus, potassium, and niacin. Mushrooms are rich sources of nucleic acids. People with gout and/or high blood levels of uric acid are advised to avoid eating mushrooms and other foods rich in nucleic acids. Wash mushrooms carefully with a brush or damp washcloth, or, if you have digestive problems, peel them.

Parsnips (Pastinaca sativa) are related to carrots and belong to the Umbelliferae or Parsely Family. They are very similar nutritionally to potatoes, although they contain only 80% the protein and Vitamin C of the potato. Choose as you would carrots. Pare parsnips (boil older parsnips for 10 mins to make this easier, and also remove their core).

Potatoes (Solanum tuberosum) are members of the Nightshade (Solanaceae) Family which includes tomatoes, peppers, and eggplant. Unfortunately, the nightshade family of vegetables is associated with increased allergenic effects and may trigger or aggrevate arthritis in particular. Only moderate use of these vegetables, if tolerated, is recommended. The potato is not related to the yam nor the sweet potato. A 200g raw potato contains about 115 Kcal, 3.2g protein, 80mg phosphorus, 1mg iron, 30mg Vitamin C, and little calcium and Vitamin A. Boiling potatoes destroys some of the Vitamin C. Baking potatoes increases the proportion of solids per weight by reducing the moisture content and, therefore, the increases the proportion of nutrients. French fried potatoes, which are even more dehydrated, contain 3-4 times the calories of boiled potatoes and every 28g of French fries also contains 5 mL of fat. When selecting potatoes, avoid those with definite green patches (caused by sun exposure) or sprouts on the surface. They may contain harmful levels of solanine, a toxic alkaloid. If you have purchased potatoes and they are now sprouting, remove the sprouts entirely.

Tomatoes (Lycopersicon esculentum) are members of the Nightshade Family (Solanaceae). As noted earlier, the Nightshades may aggravate arthritis in some people. As well, tomatoes may cause immediate-type IgE-mediated reactions in some. Monitor their introduction carefully. Tomatoes are about 94% water and are low in calories. They are a good source of Vitamins A and C. Select round, plump, firm, red tomatoes.

Pumpkins (Curcubita) are related to gourds and melons. They are high in water (90%), low in calories (30 Kcal per 100g), and an excellent source of Vitamin A.

Radishes (Raphanus sativus) are members of the Mustard Family (Cruciferae). Radish roots may be golf-ball-sized or larger (eg. the Oriental variety, Daikon, can weigh almost 2 1/2 Kg). Radishes are high in water (94%) and low in calories. Daikon radishes are lower in potassium and higher in Vitamin C than are common radishes. Choose smooth, firm radishes (older radishes may be woody). Radishes should be scrubbed (or pared if you have digestive difficulties). They may be eaten raw or steamed (this will reduce the strong flavor).

6.1.2 Cereal Grain Alternatives

These include a number of new flours. **Soy Flour**, derived from soybeans, has a "beany" flavor. **Arrowroot** is available as a flour and a starch and can be used as a thickener. Methylcellulose is another thickening agent which may be used in small quantities. **Yeast** may introduced in baking.

Buckwheat is related to rhubarb and belongs to the Polygonaceae family. It is not a cereal grain, although it is used as such. It is high in lysine and low in methionine. Buckwheat flour wheat is is free of gluten, the problematic cereal-grain proteins, but it is not a perfect wheat flour replacement. **Millet** (Panicum miliaceum) belongs to the cereal grass family (Gramineae) and can be used in a similar manner to rice. It is high in starch, and generally has more protein than the other cereal grains although it is deficient in lysine. Millet is also available as a flour. **Tapioca** is derived from the cassava root. It is used for puddings or as a binder. It also comes as a starch and a flour (best when used in combination with other flours).

Phase 4

6.1.3 Fruit

Fruit options now include dried fruit. Remember that the order of introduction is still cooked fruit, raw, juice, and finally dried fruit.

Apricots (Prunus armeniaca) are stone fruits and are close related to the almond, cherry, peach, and plum. They are about 85% water. 100g provides 51 Kcal (mostly as sugars), 319mg potassium, 2700 IU Vitamin A, and 1mg sodium. Ripe apricots are plump, golden-orange, and firm.

Blackberries (Rubus) are from the Rosaceae Family and are similar to raspberries except the blackberry core comes off with the fruit when picked. They are an excellent source of fiber, a good source of potassium and bioflavonoids (from which they get their color), and a fair to good source of folic acid and Vitamin A and C. They are fairly high in calories and carbohydrates (13%).

Cherries Sweet cherries (Prunus avium) include the common commercial variety of Bing. Sour or pie cherries are Prunus cerasus. Duke cherries are a cross between sweet and sour cherries. Sweet cherries provide 70 Kcal per 100g while sour provide only 58 Kcal (the difference being in the amount of natural sugars). Choose glossy, dark red cherries which are not withered or soft. Sour cherries are used primarily in baking, while sweet are suitable served alone or in other desserts.

Cranberries (Vaccinium) are related to blueberries and are in the Ericaceae Family. Fresh cranberries are low in calories and carbohydrates. They provide a good source of fiber and bioflavonoides (which produce their color) and a fair source of Vitamin C and potassium. Plump, fresh-looking, lusterous cranberries are best. They can be stored for months in the refrigerator.

Currants (Ribes) are related to gooseberries, members of the Saxifragaceae Family. Currants are available black, red, or white varieties. Currants provide a fair amount of calories and carbohydrates. Black currants are rich sources of fiber, Vitamin C, potassium, and bioflavonoids (the anthocyanin pigments create the color in black and red varieties) and a fair to good source of calcium, phosphorus, Vitamin A, and iron. Red and white currants, however, provide more fiber and less of all the other nutrients. Dried currants are high in calories, carbohydrates, fiber, and potassium, have some calcium and iron, but little Vitamin C. Dried currants are more readily available than fresh.

Grapes are Vitis vinifera and are classified as berries. North American grapes are "slipskin", while European are not and are more suitable for raisins. Grapes are about 80% water. They provide about 70 kcal/100 g, derived from their sugars (carbohydrate content averages 16%). Table grapes are packed after harvest, cooled, and treated with sulfur dioxide to slow decay. Allergic reactions are common. **Raisins** are dried grapes.

Mangoes (Mangifera indica) are a tropical fruit. They are about 82% water. They provide 66 Kcal per 100g. They are an excellent source of Vitamin A and a fair source of Vitamin C. Papaya (Carica papaya) is another tropical fruit. It is about 89% water and is low in calories. The fruit is rich in Vitamin A and has some Vitamin C.

Nectarines are peaches, except they lack the fuzz on the skin (see 53).

Oranges (Citrus sinensis) are members of the citrus group of fruits (lemon, lime, grapefruit). They are low in calories and provide a good source of fiber, potassium, inositol, bioflavonoids, Vitamin C, and pectin, as well as a fair source of folic acid. Fresh orange juice contains a similar profile of nutrients, but tends to have lower levels of fiber, pectin, and bioflavonoids as these are present mostly in the membranes surrounding the fruit and the peel. Undilute frozen orange juice concentrate has 3-4 times the calories of fresh juice and similar nutrient levels. Choose firm, heavy, orange-colored fruit with finely texture peel.

Pineapple (Ananas comosus) provide carbohydrate (15% sugar), vitamin A, and vitamin C. Frozen pineapple is very similar to fresh, and frozen pineapple juice is similar to fresh juice. To test a fresh pineapple for ripeness, lift it (it should be heavy with juice), press the skin at the bottom (it should be soft), and smell it (it should have a fruity fragrance).

Prunes (Prunus) are dried plums (see p. 53).

6.1.4 Fish

Fish which has red flesh (eg. **Salmon** and **Trout**) may be tried in Phase 4. Prepare it as you would whitefish. Seafood alternatives include **Abalone** and **Scallops**. Shellfish, such as **Crab**, **Lobster**, **Prawns**, and **Shrimp**, may be suitable. Immediate-type IgE-mediated allergic reactions are commonly associated with seafood ingestion; avoid crustaceans and shellfish if you have any history of allergenic effects. For a description of the nutrient profiles of fish and seafood, see p. 53.

6.1.5 Egg Substitutes

Egg Yolk is less likely to cause allergenic problems than the protein-rich egg white. However, it is rich in cholesterol and should be used for baking only. **Gelatin** is used in some baking recipes as well, as an egg substitute; it is derived from animal protein, and may be allergenic.

6.1.6 Flavorings

Flavorings in Phase 4 include small amounts of **Coconut Milk**; it is best not to consume this as a beverage. **Marshmallows** are used in a few recipes; do not use them too often and avoid the colored varieties. **Mint** may be used fresh or dried in tsp quantities or as a garnish.

Garlic, Allium sativum, belong to the lily family (Liliaceae). Garlic contains several drug-like compounds and may not be well-tolerated: Allicin, for example, retards the growth of certain bacteria; adenosine moderately well as a diuretic and a vasodilator. Fresh-cut garlic also contains an anti-clotting factor. The distinct odor is released by cutting or crushing the garlic cloves. Cooking garlic reduces the odor, allowing consumption of larger quantities. Buy only enough fresh garlic as you need and use it quickly. Chop garlic with a touch of salt to prevent it from sticking to the knife blade. Many dishes (vegetable, rice, poultry, meat, fish, tofu, seafood) are enhanced by the use of garlic.

6.2 One Dish Meals

Continue to develop combinations of basic core diet vegetables, fruit, poultry, fish, or meat options. Wok cooking remains an easy, attractive method of meal preparation.

Oriental Stir-fry

1/2 head or less Chinese, regular white, or savoy cabbage, chopped fine
4 stalks celery or bok choy, sliced 1/4" thick
1 small onion, chopped
2 carrots, thinly sliced
1 stalk broccoli, chopped
1/2 cloves garlic, minced or sliced

1/4 cup stock or water, cool
2 celery stalks, sliced diagonally
1/4 tsp salt
1/4 tsp pepper
1/4 tsp garlic powder
oil (optional)
1/4-1/3 cup tamari wheat-free soy sauce
3 tsp (or more) safe thickener

Use a non-stick frying pan (or a wok). Slowly heat the garlic (heat it with a small amount of oil if using a wok - be sure the sides of the wok are oiled). Add all the vegetables and cook until almost tender. Stir the mixture continuously to cook the vegetables completely. Mix the thickener (eg. arrowroot powder) with the water/stock and the tamari, then mix this with the vegetables. Heat everything for 1-2 mins, stir and serve.

Variations: Serve over a bed of rice...add thin slices of poultry or beef, or cubes of tofu to the stir-fry (the meats may require a slightly longer cooking time and should be added first).

P4 Chicken Hot Pot
Follow the recipes on 55, and 91 and add 1/2 cup chopped mushrooms when using onions, ginger root, and/or sesame seeds.

P4 Fried Rice
Follow the recipes on p. 36, 55, and 92 with the following adjustments.

Variations: Add 1/4 cup sliced mushrooms with the poultry...add 1/4 chopped leek with the carrot...substitute shrimp or prawns for the chicken...saute chopped garlic with the chicken or sprinkle 1/8 tsp garlic powder over the chicken.

P4 Mihoen
Follow the recipes on 56, and 92 and try the following variations.

Variations: Saute chopped garlic with the chicken or sprinkle the chicken with 1/8 tsp garlic powder...add bean sprouts, shredded cabbage or bok choy, chopped leeks, or chopped mushrooms along with or instead of the carrot...brown pineapple juice with the chicken to create a sweet sauce, then add pineapple chunks with the vermicelli. Substitute shrimp or prawns for the chicken.

Garlic prawns with seasonal vegetables

1 Tbsp oil	1/2 cup snow peas
2-3 cloves garlic	1/2 cup carrots
1/2 cup prawns	other seasonal vegetables
1/2 cup bok choy, sliced thinly	2 Tbsp soy sauce

In a non-stick skillet, heat oil and saute garlic with the prawns until almost cooked. Set aside. Stir fry vegetables adding water to steam them. When almost cooked, add prawns and soy sauce. Stir fry until well done. Serve with rice. This recipe is great with short grain white Japanese rice. Eat in small bowls with rice and dish. Also, bean sprouts can be added at the final stage of cooking.

6.3 Cooked Vegetable Dishes

P4 Stuffed Vegetables
Basic Stuffing: In addition to the foods listed on 58, and 95, you may choose to stuff the vegetable with:
- pulp from vegetable to be stuffed
- buckwheat (instead of rice)

You may use mint as a seasoning for the stuffing.

Cabbage: Wash a head of cabbage (choose one with loose leaves, rather than a solid one). Fill a dutch oven 3/4 full with water and bring it to a boil. Add the cabbage, then turn off the heat and cover for a few minutes. Using a knife, separate the leaves from the core (be careful not to burn yourself). If the inner leaves are still not pliable, soak them a little longer. Save the water. Arrange the stuffing in the middle of each leaf. Fold up the sides, then the top, and then the stem. Skewer with a toothpick or two.

Place the cabbage rolls, stem-side down, into the empty dutch oven and brown them somewhat on both sides. Add the reserved water (make sure the rolls are at least half-submerged). If you have leftover or broken cabbage leaves, chop them up and add them to the water. Bring to a boil, then simmer 30-60 mins. Or put the rolls in a baking pan with the stem-side down. Pour some of the reserved cabbage water over the rolls and bake them, covered, at 350F until heated, about 30 mins.

Beets: Steam, bake, or pressure-cook whole beets. When they are tender, scoop out the insides, leaving a shell. Mash the insides and mix with the stuffing. Stuff and bake to heat thoroughly.

Chard: Simmer chard leaves until they are wilted. Cut off the stalks (save them for future use). Follow the directions for stuffing cabbage.

Tomatoes: Cut off the tops of the tomatoes, then carefully loosen the pulp and remove it. Brush the inside of the tomatoes with a small amount of olive oil and sprinkle with salt, pepper, and herbs. Once stuffed, arrange the tomatoes in a baking dish and bake in a moderate oven 20-25 mins.

Sweet Potatoes in Coconut Milk
3 baked sweet potatoes
1 can coconut milk
brown sugar to taste

Peel and chop up the sweet potatoes. In a sauce pan, cook the sweet potatoes, coconut milk, and sugar until the sugar begins to caramelize with the milk.

Stuffed Zucchini #2

6 medium zucchini	2 tsp thyme
1 cup chopped celery	1 cup chopped mushrooms
2 cups cooked rice	salt to taste

Saute the mushrooms, celery, and thyme in a non-stick pan (or use a small amount of oil) for 5 mins. Add the rice and salt, mixing well. Cut the zucchini in half and remove the pulp. Stuff (if there is leftover stuffing, put it in the baking dish as well). Bake at 350F 30-45 mins.

Stocked Veggies
Wash carrots and slice them in ovals. Wash and slice the mushrooms. Saute the carrots in a non-stick pan (or use a small amount of oil) for 2 mins. Add the mushrooms and peas; salt to taste. Add 1/4 cup water or stock and cover; turn the heat down to medium low. Check, adding more water if necessary. Stir and continue steaming until peas are just tender.

Blaukraut

red cabbage	salt
vinegar	brown sugar
apples	pepper

Chop up the cabbage into fairly large pieces. Chop up the apples. Saute the cabbage briefly, then add the apples. Sprinkle on the brown sugar and vinegar to taste (it should be a tart, but tangy taste). Add salt and pepper to taste. Cover, cook for 5 mins for a crispy version or 20 mins for a limper version. Red cabbage can also be baked in a covered dish for 1/2 hour or more; this will be much limper than the unbaked version.

Pineappled Squash
1/2 fresh pineapple
2 acorn or butternut squash

Preheat oven to 350F. Peel the pineapple and dice it. In a small loaf pan, layer squash pieces and top with pineapple. Dot with oil and bake 30 mins.

Stir-fried Cabbage
2 1/2 cups thinly sliced cabbage
1/2 cup thinly sliced onion
pepper to taste

Heat a non-stick pan (or use a small amount of oil) and add the cabbage, stir-frying for 5 mins over medium heat or until it is just limp. Add the onion and sitr-fry for 3 mins or until it is clear and limp. Season to taste.

Boiled Chard
Use 1/2 lb chard per serving. Wash repeatedly. Cut the leaves off the stems, cooking them separately in enough boiling salted water to cover until just tender. The leaves will cook faster than the stems. When the chard is ready, drain well, chop if desired and serve with a safe dressing.

Broiled Tomatoes
1 large ripe tomato
2 tsp fresh rosemary, oregano, and/or basil, or 1/2 tsp dried freshly ground pepper to taste (optional)

Halve the tomato horizontally. Mix the herbs and the pepper (if using) and rub this mixture on the cut surface of both halves. Broil the tomatoes, cut side up, on a foil-lined pan until very hot (about 5-8 mins).

Marinated Zucchini

3 large zucchini	1 tsp chopped fresh or 1/2 tsp
1/2 tbsp olive oil	oregano
3 tbsp lemon juice	1 tbsp chopped parsley
3 tsp vinegar	1/2 clove garlic, minced

Trim the zucchini (or another type of summer squash) and cut it lengthwise into thin slices. Mix the oil, lemon juice, and garlic and let it stand. Brush half of the oil mixture over the zucchini. Heat a nonstick skillet over moderate heat. Stir-fry the zucchini, about 1 min on each side, until golden. Put the zucchini in a shallow dish. Add the vinegar and oregano to the remaining oil mixture and pour this over the zucchini. Let this stand at least 1 hr. Sprinkle the parsley over the zucchini just before serving.

Tomatoed Green Beans

6 tbsp safe chicken stock	4 peeled tomatoes, diced
1 lb string beans, trimmed and	salt and pepper to taste
washed	chopped parsley
	pinch safe dried herbs

Combine stock and tomatoes; bring to a boil. Add the beans and herbs; cover and simmer until the beans are almost tender. Remove the lid and simmer until any excess liquid has evaporated. Sprinkle with salt, pepper, and parsley.

Marinated Leeks

Poach 12-14 leeks until just tender in enough safe chicken/beef broth or water to cover. Or put the leeks and stock/water in a microwavable dish and cover with plastic wrap; cook about 10-12 mins on full power. Drain and cool the leeks (save the broth for a soup). Marinate, chilled, for several hours in a safe vinaigrette sauce.

6.4 Salads

A new variety of vegetables and fruits may now be added to your salads: shredded cabbage, cooked diced or raw-grated beets, cooked diced pumpkin, minced mint leaves, chopped radishes, diced pineapple, currants or raisins, chopped mushrooms, and grapes.

Cabbage Salad
Combine fresh diced pineapple, shredded red cabbage, and chopped parsley. Toss with a safe vinaigrette dressing (see p. 139.

Cole Slaw
1 green cabbage, shredded
1 red cabbage, shredded

1 onion, finely chopped
3 carrots, grated

Bring Cole Slaw Dressing (see p. 100) ingredients to a boil. Combine the vegetables and pour the dressing over the mixture. Cover and chill overnight.

Crunchy Salad
6-8 leaves leaf lettuce
1/2 cup red cabbage

green onions or chives (optional)
1-2 stalks celery

Shred the lettuce and cabbage. Chop the celery and green onions/chives (if using). Combine all the ingredients. Toss with your favorite safe dressing.

Creamy Surprise Salad
Slice mushrooms and carrots. Add to shredded lettuce. Add diced pineapple and pumpkin seeds. Toss with a creamy dressing (see p. 139).

Oriental Chicken Salad
2 tbsp tamari wheat-free soy sauce
1 firm, ripe tomato, peeled, seeded, and cut into wedges
2 tsp olive oil
1 tsp packed brown sugar
1 clove garlic, finely chopped
6 large mushrooms, sliced

pepper
1 small zucchini, sliced
2 whole chicken breasts (3/4 lb each), boned, skinned
1 stalk celery, sliced
1 small carrot, sliced
1/2 cup trimmed snow peas
8 cups lettuce or spinach

Combine the soy sauce, oil, brown sugar, garlic, and pepper in a large bowl. Cut the chicken into thin strips. Add the chicken to the marinade, making sure to coat it. Cover and chill 2 hours. Remove chicken. Simmer the marinade in a small saucepan. Heat a large non-stick skillet over high heat. Add the chicken and all the vegetables except the snow peas and greens. Stir-fry 8 mins. Add the snow peas, stir-frying 1 min. In a serving bowl, toss the lettuce with the warm marinade, then top with the chicken mixture.

Potato Salad
5 medium potatoes

3 stalks celery, chopped

4 green onions, chopped   1 medium apple, chopped
                               1 tbsp lemon juice

Boil the potatoes until just tender, drain, and cool. Peel the potates and cut into cubes. Combine with the remaining ingredients, toss with Mustard Dressing, and chill prior to serving.

Pineapple Salad
Halve a fresh pineapple. Scoop out the center. Mix this scooped out pineapple with crabmeat and diced celery and apple. Fill the center of the pineapple halves with this mixture.

Basic Millet Salad
Follow a rice salad recipe (eg. p. 97) and substitute cooked millet for the rice.

6.4.1 Salad Dressings and Dips

If you are concerned about dietary fat, in Phase 4 you may dress raw vegetables with lemon juice and herbs.

Mayonnaise
2 egg yolks   1 cup oil
1 tsp dry mustard   2 tbsp hot water
                               2 tsp lemon juice

Blend the egg yolks, mustard, and lemon juice until smooth. Add the oil gradually. Add enough water to achieve the desired consistency.

Mustard Dressing
2 tbsp vinegar   1/4 tsp dry mustard
1/3 cup olive oil   2 tsp sugar
2 tsp lemon juice   1 clove garlic, crushed

Combine all the ingredients, stirring well.

Fruit Juice Dressing
2/3 cup sugar   2 tbsp lemon juice
1/3 cup water   2 tbsp lime juice
                               2 tbsp orange juice

Strain the juices to remove the pulp. Mix the strained juice with the water and sugar, stirring until the sugar dissolves.

Chickpea-Tahini Spread
See p. 162.

Pineapple Dip
1 medium pineapple, diced
2 tsp grated ginger root
1/2 cup chopped fresh mint

Mix all the ingredients, refrigerate, and serve.

Lemon/Lime Spark
Use freshly squeezed lemon or lime juice over cooked vegetables. For variety, add chopped chives, parsley, mint leaves (fresh), dill, or a very small amount of crushed garlic.

6.5 Rice, Millet and Buckwheat Dishes

P4 Rice and Carrots
Follow the recipes on p. 28 , 65, and 100, and try the following:

Variations: Add cooked vegetables from Phase 4, stirring them into the rice when it has finished cooking...substitute buckwheat or millet for the Uncle Ben's converted white rice.

Raisin-Basmati Pilaf

2 tbsp shredded coconut	3 1/2 cups water
750g Basmati rice	1/2 tbsp safe oil
650 mL coconut milk	1/2 cup raisins
	2 tbsp sesame seeds

In a heavy pan, over medium heat, lightly toast the coconut. Remove from the pan and cool. Wash the rice and mix it with the coconut milk and water in a large saucepan. Stir this over medium heat and bring to a boil. Add the raisins, reduce the heat, cover partially, and simmer for about 10 mins (until most of the liquid is absorbed). Cover and simmer over low heat for 10 more mins. Remove from heat, but leave covered. Heat the oil and roast the sesame seeds over medium heat until they are lightly browned. Stir the seeds into the rice mixture. To serve, sprinkle the rice with coconut.

Prunes and Rice
Add 1/2 cup chopped, pitted prunes to rice as it cooks.

6.5.1 Buckwheat and Millet Dishes

Cooking Buckwheat and Millet

Rinse the grain in cold water and drain well. Bring water/stock to a boil. Add the grain slowly, stirring, and add salt (1/4-1/2 tsp per cup of grain). Boil again, then turn the heat down to low. Cook slowly until all the liquid is absorbed (see below for cooking times). If the grain still seems hard or tough, add a little boiling water, cover, and continue cooking. Do not stir it any more than necessary, or it will be gummy.

COOKING TIMES (for 1 cup grain, dry measure)
Buckwheat - 2 cups water - 1 hr - yield 2 1/2 cups
Millet - 3 cups water - 45 mins - yield 3 1/2 cups}

Variations: Combine grains (remember to take into account differences in cooking times) and stir ground toasted sesame seeds into cooked grain.

Buckwheat and White Rice

Combine 3 parts uncooked rice with 1 part buckwheat. Cook as per rice.

Buckwheat Groats #1

1/2 cup raw buckwheat groats
1 1/4 cups water or stock with an another 1/4 cup reserved

Put the groats and 1 1/4 cups water into a small saucepan. Bring to a boil, then reduce the heat and simmer until tender (3-5 mins), stirring occasionally. (Add the reserved 1/4 cup liquid if needed during simmering).

Buckwheat Groats #2

Use 1 part grain to 2 parts water and 1/4 tsp salt per cup of grain. Put all the ingredients in a pan, cover and bring to a boil. Reduce the heat and simmer 20 mins.

Variation: Saute the grain in a non-stick pan (or use a small amount of oil) before adding it to boiling water, then reduce the simmering time to 10-15 mins.

Buckwheat is available as a grain and as a flour (see 151 for recipes).

Millet Casserole

1/2 lb millet	1 carrot, chopped
2 onions, diced	2 cloves garlic, minced
2 1/2 cups water/stock	1 cup sliced mushrooms
1/2 tbsp oil	

Preheat the oven to 350F. Brown the millet in a frying pan and remove. Fry the garlic and onions. Combine the garlic, onions, browned millet, carrots, and stock in a casserole dish. Cover and bake until the millet is tender, about 2 hours.

Millet Cereal
See p. 142. Boiled millet can be used as a side dish for stews and casseroles.

Millet Groats
Substitute millet for buckwheat in the Buckwheat Groats #2 recipe (p. 141).

Millet-Rice Pilaf
1 medium onion, chopped
1 cup long grain rice

3/4 cup hulled millet
1 1/2 cups safe stock
1 cup cooked green peas

Saute the onion in a non-stick saucepan (or use a little oil) over medium heat. Add the rice and millet, stirring to coat them with oil if using. Add the stock and bring to a boil. Reduce the heat, cover tightly, and simmer for 12 mins. Remove from the heat, add the peas, and cover tightly. Let stand 15 mins, then stir and serve.

6.6 Breakfast

Cereal breakfasts now include buckwheat (hot cereal) and millet (both puffed and as hot cereal). Pancakes and waffles can be made from non-wheat flours such as buckwheat, soy, and arrowroot.

P4 ProSobee Waffles
Follow the Phase 3 recipe (p. 93), substituting 1 cup of another non-wheat flour (or combination of flours) of your choice for the rice flour.

Rice Flour Pancakes #5
1 cup rice flour
2 tbsp oil

2 egg yolks
1 1/2 tsp baking powder
1 cup soy milk

Mix the dry ingredients together. Make a well in the middle and add the liquid ingredients. Mix. Ladle the batter onto a hot oiled frying pan and fry pancakes until done, turning once.

Variations: Add 1/4 cup currants, cubed sliced peaches, or safe fruit salad to the batter...substitute 1/4 rice polish for 1/4 cup rice flour...substitute 3/4 cup other non-wheat flour for 3/4 rice flour.

Buckwheat Pancakes #1

1 3/4 cups water	1/2 tsp salt
1 tbsp sugar	blueberries or raspberries
1 3/4 cups buckwheat	1/4 cup oil

Mix the ingredients together and cook on a well-oiled, hot griddle, turning once.

Buckwheat Pancakes #2

1 cup buckwheat flour	1 tsp salt
1 tsp oil	2 tsp baking powder
	1 1/4 cup water

Mix all the ingredients, stirring well. Beat until foamy. Fry the pancakes in a well-oiled frying pan, watching carefully that they do not burn.

Buckwheat Pancakes #3

1 1/2 cups buckwheat
3/4 cup arrowroot
about 1 1/2 cups water

Grind the buckwheat to make a fine flour. Mix it with the arrowroot. Stir in the water, adding enough to make pancake batter consistency to make a good pouring consistency. Pour a small amount of batter into an oiled pan. Fry well on both sides.

Buckwheat Pancakes #4

1 cup buckwheat flour	3/4 tsp cream of tartar
3 tbsp melted milk-free margarine	1 1/2-2 cups boiling water
	1/2 tsp baking soda

Sift the flour, cream of tartar, and baking soda together in a large mixing bowl. Pour the melted margarine into the flour, mixing well. Slowly add 1 1/2 cups boiling water, stirring constantly, to make a smooth batter (add up to 1/2 cup more boiling water if necessary). The batter should be thick. Heat a non-stick frying pan. Use 3 tbsp batter per pancake, spreading the batter out to make a thin pancake. Reduce the heat, cooking the pancakes until the edges brown and air bubbles appear in the centers

(about 5-6 mins). Turn the pancakes when they can slide in the pan and cook until the center springs back when touched (about 3-4 mins).
Blueberry Buckwheat Pancakes: Stir in 3/4 cup fresh blueberries after adding the water.

ProSobee Pancakes

1/2 cup ProSobee Ready-to-Use	2 tbsp oil
2 tbsp cornstarch	1 1/2 tsp baking powder
1/2 cup water	1 cup sifted rice flour
1/2 tsp salt	2 tbsp sugar

Combine liquid ingredients and blend in dry ingredients, stirring until the mixture is smooth. Heat an oiled frying pan and cook the pancakes (make them small), turning once.

Arrowroot Pancakes

1 cup seeds	1 1/2 tbsp oil
1/2 cup arrowroot starch	2 tsp baking powder
1 cup water	2 tbsp honey

Using a blender, puree seeds of your choice with the water. Combine with the remaining ingredients, mixing well. Follow Cooking Non-Wheat Flour Pancakes instructions to cook.

P4 Granola
See p. 164.

Buckwheat Cereal
1/2 cup buckwheat
1 cup water

Combine and simmer 30 mins, until tender.

Millet Cereal
3 1/4 - 3 1/2 cups water
1 cup millet

Bring water to a boil. Simmer gently 30 mins. (Soak overnight to hasten cooking). Sweeten with canned peaches/pears and juice.

6.7 Soups, Stocks, and Appetizers

6.7.1 Soups

P4 Chicken Soup
Follow the recipes on 67 with the following variations.

Variations: Add bok choy and/or cabbage to the soup or use one or both instead of carrots and/or broccoli...add papaya to the soup or use it instead of squash...instead of rice, use diced potatoes, adding them with the other vegetables...saute chopped garlic with the poultry.

P4 Grain Soup
Follow the Phase 1 recipe (p. 37) and substitute 1 cup buckwheat for the rice.

P4 Squash Soup
Follow the Phase 1 and 2 recipes (see p. 38 and 67), adding leeks, mushrooms, and chard to your list of ingredients from which to choose. If you use chard, do not saute it; add it 4-5 mins before serving.

Potato Soup: Substitute 4 medium potatoes for the squash.

P4 Leftover Turkey Soup
Follow the recipe on p. 67 and add 1 clove garlic, minced (saute it with the onion) and/or 1/2 cup finely chopped mushrooms (add them with the carrots and celery).

P4 Turkey Vegetable Soup
Follow the Phase 2 recipe (p. 67) and substitute 1/4 cup millet flour for the rice flour and/or adding 1 cup chopped mushrooms.

P4 Split Pea Soup
Follow the Phase 3 recipe (p. 101) adding 2 cloves of garlic, minced, to be sauted with the onion, and/or 1 cup diced potato, added to the soup with the stock, tamari, and pepper.

P4 Melon Soup
Follow the recipe on p. 4.7 and add lemon juice for added flavor. You may also substitute a safe Phase 4 fruit juice for the water or Phase 4 fruit for the melon. Garnish the soup with chopped mint or lemon/lime slices.

Microwaved Vegetable Soup

1/2 cup diced turnip
1 tbsp safe oil
4 cups beef stock
1 large carrot, diced
1/2 cup rice
1 leek finely sliced
1/2 cup water
1 tbsp tomato paste

1 stalk chopped celery
1 cup shredded cabbage
1/4 tsp salt
1 cup chopped onion
1/4 tsp garlic powder
2 cups chopped tomatoes
1/4 tsp pepper
1/4 tsp rosemary

Place oil, turnip, carrot, leek, celery, onion, cabbage, tomatoes, and water into a 3 qt microwavable casserole dish. Cover and microwave 10-12 mins on high, stirring once. Heat the beef stock, then stir it, the tomato paste, rice, and seasonings into the vegetable mixture. Cover and microwave 15-20 mins on medium, stirring once. Let stand 2-4 mins before serving.

Lentil Soup

5 cups or more chicken stock
1/2 tsp dried basil
3 cups or more water
1/2 tsp dried oregano
1 1/2 cups lentils
1/2 tsp dried thyme
1 bay leaf
1 cup long-grain brown rice

1/2 cup minced parsley
1 35-oz can tomatoes
2 tbsp vinegar, or to taste
3 carrots, chopped
salt (optional) to taste
pepper to taste
1 cup chopped onion
1/2 cup chopped celery
1 tbsp minced garlic

Combine the stock, water, lentils, rice, canned tomatoes (chopped with juice), carrots, onion, celery, garlic, basil, oregano, thyme, and bay leaf in a Dutch oven. Bring to a boil, then cover and simmer, stirring occasionally, until the rice and lentils are tender (45-55 mins). Discard the bay leaf. The soup can be frozen at this stage. Stir in the parsley, vinegar, salt, and pepper. To thin the soup, add more hot stock/water.

Pumpkin Soup

6 cups safe chicken stock
2 lbs pumpkin,
2 medium onions, chopped

salt (optional) to taste
1 cup soy milk or ProSobee
1 tbsp thickener
1/4 cup cold water

In a large saucepan, heat the stock. Peel and cut the pumpkin into 1-inch cubes and add onions, and salt. Cook until the pumpkin is soft, about 20 mins. Puree the soup, a little at a time, in a blender or food processor, or force the soup through a sieve. (The soup base can be frozen at this stage if desired). Return the soup to the pan. Mix the thickener and water, stirring until the mixture is smooth. Add this mixture to the soup; heat the soup, stirring, until it boils. Add the soy milk and season to taste. Serve alone or with rice bread croutons.

Borscht

2-3 beets	carrots, cabbage, or other safe
1/2 tsp fresh dill	vegetable of choice, in quantity
1 onion	equivalent to beets
salt to taste	24 fl oz stock or water

Saute the vegetables in a non-stick pan for about 15 mins. Add the stock/water and simmer until the vegetables are tender. Season and simmer 10 more mins (thicken with 1 tbsp soy flour if desired). For a smooth soup, puree in a blender and reheat before serving. For a chunky soup, cube the vegetables and do not blend.

Grain Soup #2

3/4 cup buckwheat	diced celery
5-6 cups water/stock	other diced safe vegetables of
diced carrots	choice

Wash the grain and discard the water. Simmer the grain in water or stock for 1 hour or longer, adding the vegetables after about 1/2 hour (or saute them in a non-stick pan for 5 mins and add them to the soup after 45-50 mins). Season to taste with safe herbs and salt.

6.7.2 Appetizers

Stuffed Celery #2
4 oz. tofu
1/4 cup crushed pineapple
1 tsp safe herb

Mix together and stuff celery sticks.

Stuffed Mushrooms
Use any combination of safe vegetables or meats to stuff mushroom caps. Broil, watching carefully that they do not burn.

Seafood Cocktail
Use a combination of seafood and vegetables of your choice:

prawns/shrimp	diced celery
oysters	sliced cucumber
crab	chopped green onion
scallops	other safe vegetable slices

Serve with a creamy dressing (see p. 139) on a bed of shredded lettuce.

6.8 Advanced Entrees

Chicken Stuffed with Brown Rice

1 1/2 lb whole chicken	1/2 cup steamed brown rice
2 cups water/stock	1/2 cup mushrooms

Wash and chop mushrooms; mix the pieces with the cooked rice. Wash the chicken and stuff it slightly over half full, allowing room for expansion. Heat a large non-stick saucepan (or use a small amount of oil in a wok). Brown both sides of the chicken, then add the water/stock. Bring to a boil, then simmer until tender (about 1 1/2 hours), turning frequently to cook evenly.

Skillet Chicken

3 cups chicken stock	2 lbs green cabbage, cored and thinly sliced
2 lbs carrots, peeled and sliced lengthwise	1 chicken (about 3-4 lbs), cut into pieces and skinned
2 tsp sugar	3 large onions, thinly sliced
salt (optional) to taste	1 tbsp minced garlic
	safe herbs if desired

Bring the stock to a boil in a medium pot. Add the carrots, sugar, and salt. Simmer, covered, for 1/2 hour. Meanwhile, boil the cabbage (salt the water if desired) for 5 mins, then drain it. Season the chicken pieces on both sides with safe herbs (if using). Brown the chicken in a large non-stick skilet (or use a small amount of oi). Remove the chicken and saute the onions and garlic for about 5 mins. Add the cabbage and saute 3 more mins. Add the chicken, cover, and simmer 35 mins. Add the carrots and stock. Bring to a boil, uncovered, to reduce the liquid.

Phase 4

Turkey Cabbage Rolls
Mix ground turkey, salt to taste, and finely diced dill (Advanced) with a small amount of cooked rice. Use this as stuffing for cabbage leaves (see Stuffed Vegetables p. 134). Skewer each cabbage roll with a toothpick. Place the rolls in a large pot and add water/stock or chopped tomatoes plus water/stock until the rolls are 1/2-3/4 submerged. Bring to a boil, then simmer, turning occasionally, until the meat is cooked and the cabbage is tender. Thicken the liquid if desired (see gravy recipes p. 164) and serve the rolls with gravy. Serve on a bed of rice.

Lemon Chicken
1 fryer chicken (about 3 lbs) cut up and skinned
2 tbsp chopped fresh or 2 tsp dried rosemary
1 tsp pepper
juice of 2 lemons
1 clove garlic, minced

Combine the lemon juice, rosemary, pepper, and garlic and marinate the chicken in this for 2 hours or more. Heat the Broiler or barbecue and cook the chicken, turning occasionally, until throughly cooked, about 25 mins.

Chicken Cacciatore
2 tsp oil
2 cups (1 lb) chopped tomatoes
1/2 cup chopped onion
2 tsp sliced garlic
1/2 bay leaf
1/4 cup chopped fresh parsley

3 tbsp fresh or 1 tsp dried basil
2 lbs chicken, chopped into pieces
1 carrot, sliced
2 cups safe chicken stock
1 stalk celery, sliced
pepper to taste

Heat a casserole dish until warm and add the oil. Saute the onion for 1 min. Add the garlic and parsley, sauteing for 1/2 min. Add the chicken and brown on all sides. Add the stock, tomatoes, and herbs; mix well. Add the carrot and celery. Bring to a boil for 1 min, then simmer for 2 hours, stirring occasionally. Skim the fat off. Season to taste with pepper. Serve immediately over rice or rice noodles.

P4 Poached Fish
Follow the Phase 2 recipe on p. 72 and substitute salmon or trout for whitefish. Add 1 bay leaf and/or 3 slices of lemon with the onion.

Fancy Cod
Bake or fry cod fillets. Place them on a bed of steamed shredded cabbage. Pour a line of squash-rice sauce down the center of the fillets.

Fancy Salmon

Follow the recipe for Fancy Cod (above) and substitute a cucumber or broccoli pureed vegetable sauce for the squash-rice sauce.

Microwave Fish Casserole

1 tbsp safe oil
1 lb whitefish fillets
1/2 cup chopped onion
28 oz can tomatoes

1/2 cup chopped celery
1/2 cup white rice
1/4 tsp salt
1/4 tsp garlic powder

Oil a microwavable casserole (sides too) and heat for 4-5 mins on high. Add the onion and celery. Cover and microwave on high for 2-3 mins. Add the rice, garlic powder, salt, and tomatoes (chop up the tomatoes with a spoon). Cover and microwave on high for 6 mins. Stir well. Put the fish on top of the rice. Cover and microwave on high until the rice is tender (about 8 mins).

Sesame Salmon

6 fresh salmon fillets
1 tsp honey
3 tbsp toasted sesame seeds

2 tbsp vinegar
2 green onions thinly sliced
1 clove garlic, crushed
2 tbsp oil

Mix the garlic, honey, vinegar, and 1 tbsp oil together in a shallow pan. Add the salmon, coating well; marinate for 2 hrs. Remove the salmon and pat dry. Heat a non-stick skillet (or use the other tbsp oil) and saute the salmon over medium-high heat until just cooked through. Sprinkle with toasted sesame seeds from marinade and pat dry. Heat the remaining 1 tbsp sesame oil in a nonstick skillet over medium-high heat. Add salmon and saute, turning once, until the fish is just cooked through, about 3 mins on each side. Sprinkle fish with the green onion and toasted sesame seeds (heat the seeds in a skillet over medium-low heat, stirring often, until they turn golden).

P4 Meatballs

Follow the Phase 2 and 3 recipes on p. 73 and 104, substituting 2 tbsp millet meal for the rice...add 1 1/2 tsp minced fresh mint or crumbled dry mint.

Cabbage Rolls

Mix equal parts raw ground beef with cooked rice. Add sauted onion if desired. Follow the p. 148 recipe.

Lamb Meatballs
Follow the P4 Meatballs recipe (p. 150), substituting ground lean lamb for the beef.

Apricot Glazed Lamb
Heat 1/4 cup Apple Jelly (see p. 81) until melted. Add chopped mint if desired. Stir in 2 jars Heinz strained apricot baby food. Roast as per Roast Lamb on p. 74, brushing the lamb with glaze every 15 mins. Do not make a gravy; instead serve the remaining glaze as a sauce.

Lamb Zucchini
1/2 lb coarsely ground lean lamb	8 small zucchini, trimmed
1 medium onion, minced	1 tbsp olive oil
	2 cups tomato sauce
	water

Preheat the oven to 400F. Heat a non-stick skillet over medium heat (or use a small amount of oil); saute the lamb with the onion, and seasonings until the lamb is lightly browned. Remove everything from pan, draining with a slotted spoon. Heat the same skillet moderately (add the 1 tbsp oil if using). Cook the zucchini whole, turning them, until they are slightly soft (about 12 mins). Put the zucchini into a large casserole and make a lengthwise slit almost completely through to bottom of each. Stuff with the lamb mixture (spoon leftovers on top). Cover with the tomato sauce. Add enough water to barely cover the zucchini. Cover with foil and bake 40-50 mins or until the lamb and squash are tender.

Lemon Lamb Chops
Use the marinade from Lemon Chicken (p. 149) for trimmed lamb chops.

6.9 BAKING

6.9.1 Breads

Pumpkin Apricot Bread
Double the Pumpkin Apricot Muffin recipe (p. 156) and bake as loaves.

Plain Rice Bread
1 cup cooked rice	2 tsp baking powder
1 tsp salt	1/2 cup rice polish
1 cup rice flour	4 egg yolks

2 tsp guar gum

4 1/2 tsp oil
2 cups water

Preheat oven to 350F. Mix all the ingredients together; the mixture should be fairly stiff. Place it into an oiled loaf pan or casserole. Bake 50-60 mins. Serve toasted (Note: Like store-bought rice bread, this bread generally takes twice as long to toast as wheat bread).

Flavored Rice Bread

1 1/4 cups rice flour
1 cup + 2-4 tbsp water
4 egg yolks
3 tbsp oil

3/4 cup soy milk or ProSobee powder
1 tbsp sugar
1/2 tsp salt
2 1/2 tsp baking powder
1/2 cup cooked vegetables

Preheat oven to 350F. Mix together dry ingredients. Pour the liquid ingredients into a well in the middle of the dry ingredients and mix. This mixture should not be too stiff nor too runny. Spoon into an oiled loaf pan. Bake 45-50 mins. Turn out on rack when done. This will not rise to the top of the pan; the bread is like an loaf cake with half-sized slices. Serve sliced, toasting in a toaster oven (do not use a regular toaster). Wrap the bread as soon as it cools, as it dries out quickly. Store/freeze in double plastic bags.

Variations: Substitute any combination of buckwheat or millet flours for some or all of the rice flour...substitute washed currants, seeds, or grated raw vegetables for the cooked vegetables.

Cooked Rice Bread

1 cup cooked rice
1 tsp salt
1 cup rice flour
2 tsp baking powder
1/2 cup rice polish

4 egg yolks
4 tbsp soy milk or ProSobee powder
4 1/2 tbsp oil
2 cups water or vegetable juice

Preheat oven to 350F. Mix all ingredients in a medium-sized bowl. Put the mixture into an oiled loaf pan or casserole. Bake for 50-60 mins.

Variation: Add 1/2 cup cooked or grated raw vegetables to the batter (eg. cooked squash, chopped cooked or raw broccoli).

Rice Bread with Yeast

6 cups short-grain rice flour
1/2 cup warm water

1/4 cup oil
2 2/3 cups water

4 tsp yeast	2 tbsp honey
1 tbsp salt (less if desired)	1/4 cup methylcellulose

The night before, mix rice flour, 2 2/3 cups water, and salt in a mixer on low or by hand. Let stand. The next morning or 12 hours later, mix together 1/2 cup water, oil, yeast, and honey. Proof yeast 10 mins. After mixing rice flour again, add yeast mixture to it (if using instant yeast, add immediately to mixed rice flour, as per instructions). Mix vigorously, then add 1/4 cup methylcellulose and mix again. Batter will be very stiff and thick, but not like wheat bread dough. Spoon into 2 well-oiled and floured loaf pans. Wet hands and pat down to smooth the top. Let rise uncovered in a warm place. Watch carefully and when dough reaches top of pan and/or small pinholes appear (about 40 mins), bake in preheated oven (375-400F) for 40 mins. Remove from pan when baked. Do not slice warm. Cool and freeze; slice when nearly frozen and store in the freezer. The rising time seems to be critical; the dough can go from perfection to disaster in 5-10 mins, so watch carefully after 30-35 mins.

Oven Rice Bread

3 cups rice flour	1 tsp salt
1/3 cup soy milk powder	1 egg yolk + 2 tbsp water
1/4 cup sugar (or to taste)	1/3 cup melted milk-free
2 cups water	margarine
	6 tsp baking powder

Preheat the oven to 375F. Sift the flour into a mixing bowl and add the sugar, salt, and baking powder. In another bowl, dissolve the soy milk powder in the water and add the egg + water and the melted margarine. Gradually add the liquid ingredients to the dry, stirring gently (do not overmix). Pour the batter into a loaf pan (to make an 8 1/2" x 4 1/2" loaf). Brush the top with more melted safe shortening and let it rest for 5 mins. Before placing the pan in the oven, cover it loosely with aluminum foil that has been pierced 2-3 times to let out steam. Bake 30 mins, remove the foil, reduce the heat to 350F and bake 45 mins longer. Test with a toothpick (it should come out clean and dry); if the loaf is not ready, return the pan to the oven for 10 more mins. Remove the pan from the oven. This loaf is moist and fragile when hot, so remove it carefully from the pan and cool it on a wire rack. Slice the loaf and store in plastic. Serve warm (toast it or heat it in the oven).

Variation: Substitute 2 small egg yolks or 1 large egg yolk for the soy milk powder.

Soy Milk Rice Bread

3 cups rice flour	1/3 cup ProSobee powder
1/4 cup sugar	2 cups water
2 tbsp baking powder	1 egg yolk + 1 tsp water
1 tsp salt	1/3 cup + 1 tsp safe oil

Mix together the flour, salt, sugar, and baking powder in a large bowl. Mix the ProSobee and water in another bowl. Add the egg yolk + water and 1/3 cup oil to the ProSobee. Gradually stir the liquid ingredients into the dry until just blended. Pour the batter into an oiled loaf pan. Brush the top with 1 tsp oil. Let stand 5 mins. Poke 2 or 3 holes into a piece of tinfoil and use this to cover the pan loosely. Bake at 375F for 30 mins. Remove the foil and turn the oven down to 350F. Bake for 45 mins more or until a toothpick inserted into the center of the loaf comes out clean. Carefully remove the loaf from the pan to a wire rack (the bread is quite crumbly when hot). This bread is best served warm.

Pancake Breads #1

2 cups brown rice flour	3 cups water
1/2 cup soy flour	1/2 tsp salt

Mix all the ingredients (you may have to keep stirring the mixture up as you go). Spoon the batter onto a small hot non-stick frying pan (or use a small amount of oil). Spread the batter very thinly. Make one flatbread at a time, turning it carefully when it appears to have dried out a bit.

Pancake Breads #2

1/2 cup buckwheat/millet flour	2 tsp oil
1/2 cup brown rice/tapioca flour	2 tsp arrowroot powder
1/3-2/3 cup extra flour for kneading	1/2 cup water

Sift the flours and the arrowroot powder together. Mix the oil and water together and add this to the dry ingredients, using a fork and then your hands. Knead the mixture, adding extra flour if necessary, then roll the dough into a ball. Divide it into 8 pieces. Roll each piece into a ball and flatten it by hand. Then use a floured rolling pin and roll each piece between 2 sheets of floured wax paper, turning frequently. Heat a non-stick frying pan (or use a small amount of oil). Preheat the oven to 400F. Put a thin pancake bread in the frying pan, heating it 15-20 seconds per side. Then put it immediately into the oven (on the rack). Bake it for 3 mins on one side, then turn it over for 1 1/2-2 mins. Re-oil the frying pan before heating each bread if necessary (use a paper towel dipped in oil). Serve hot or cold. Cool the breads before storing them in plastic bags.

Herb Bread

3/4 cup rice flour	1/2 tsp basil
1 clove garlic	2 tsp baking powder
1/4 cup soy flour	1-2 tbsp fresh parsley
1 tsp oregano	3 tbsp oil
2 tbsp tapioca pudding	3-4 tbsp sesame seeds

Mix together all dry ingredients and herbs. Mix in the oil with a fork. Oil a large pan. Add the water to the mixture (adjusting to achieve desired texture). Pour the mixture into the pan, as if to make 4 pancakes. Sprinkle with sesame seeds. Bake at 400F for 20-30 mins.

6.9.2 Dumplings

Boiled Dumplings

3/4 cup rice flour or 1/2 cup rice flour + 1/4 cup buckwheat 1 1/2 scoops ProSobee milk powder	1 1/4 tsp baking powder 1 egg yolk + water 1 tsp seeds/herbs (optional) 1/4 tsp salt

Put all dry ingredients into a bowl. Place the egg yolk in a measuring cup and add enough water to make 1/2 cup. Make a well in the middle of the dry ingredients and add the liquid ingredients. Stir together; the dough should be quite stiff. Place 3 cups of water, vegetable water, or thin soup in a pot
with a lid; bring to a boil. Drop dumplings by heaping teaspoonful into the boiling liquid, leaving space in between each dumpling. Simmer, covered, 15-20 mins. Poke dumplings with a toothpick; if it comes out clean, they are done. Ladle the dumplings out and serve with soup or stew. Leftover cooked dumplings should be cooled and immediately put into 2 plastic bags or double-wrapped with Saran wrap and stored in the fridge. Makes 8-9 dumplings.

6.9.3 Biscuits

Buckwheat Drop Biscuits

2 cups buckwheat flour	1 tsp salt
2 tbsp oil	1 cup water

Preheat the oven to 350F. Sift the dry ingredients together, then, using your hands, add the oil. Gradually add the water. A thick batter will form. Drop this by teaspoonful onto a cookie sheet and bake 25 mins.

Egged Rice Biscuits
1 1/2 cups white or brown rice flour
2 egg yolks + water
2 1/2 tsp baking powder
1/2 tsp salt
3 scoops of ProSobee powder
1 tsp seeds/herbs (optional)

Put all dry ingredients into a bowl. Place egg yolks into a measuring cup and add enough water to make 1 cup. Make a well in the middle of the dry ingredients and add the liquid ingredients. Mix; the dough should be quite stiff (if not stiff enough, add another tbsp or more of flour). Shape into 4 balls. Place on an oiled pan. Cook at 350F for 15-20 mins. Makes 4 biscuits. These do not last more than 2 days (they turn hard). To reheat them in an oven, place them in a foil pouch with a sprinkle of water and seal, placing the pouch in a preheated 350F oven for 10-15 mins. To reheat them in a microwave, wrap them in a piece of paper towel and heat for 30-40 seconds.

Variation: Substitute 1/2 cup buckwheat or millet flour for 1/2 cup rice flour.

6.9.4 Muffins

Pumpkin Apricot Muffins
Follow the recipe for Peachy Rice Muffins (p. 79) and substitute 1/2 cup cooked pumpkin for the squash and diced canned apricots for the canned peaches. These muffins can also be made without the canned apricots.

Combo Flour Muffins
2 cups non-wheat flour(s)
1/2 cup sugar
1 1/2 cups soy milk or fruit juice
4 egg yolks + extra soy milk, juice, or water
2 tsp cream of tartar
1 tsp salt
1 tsp vanilla
1/2 cup soft milk-free margarine
1 1/2 tsp baking soda

Put all ingredients into a large bowl. Mix well, until light and whipped. Batter may appear very wet when mixed. Heat oven to 300F. Fill muffin cups 3/4 full. Bake 25 mins, until just done (test with a fork). Allow muffins to cool before removing them from the tin, as they stick.

Carob Muffins: Add 3 level tbsp carob powder to the batter.

Carrot Muffins: Add 1 cup grated carrots to the batter.

Carrot-Zucchini Muffins: Add 1/2 cup grated carrots and 1/2 cup grated zucchini to the batter.

Blueberry Muffins: Add 1 cup frozen or fresh blueberries to the batter.

Rice Cereal Muffins

1/4 cup milk-free margarine	1 tsp salt
2 tbsp baking powder	1 cup rice flour
1/4 cup sugar	1/4 cup cornstarch
1 cup ProSobee liquid	1 cup water
	1 cup rice cereal

Preheat the oven to 400F. Beat the shortening, sugar, salt, cornstarch, and baking powder together until smooth and creamy. Alternately beat in the ProSobee liquid and rice flour until smooth. Stir in the water. Add the rice cereal and stir. Fill oiled muffin tins 2/3 full. Bake until brown, 25-30 mins.

Rice Muffins with Yeast
Follow the Rice Bread with Yeast recipe (p. 152), using muffin tins instead of loaf pans.

Brown Rice Flakes Muffins

1 1/2 cups brown rice flour	2 egg yolks + 2 tsp water
1/2 cup rice polish or rice bran	1/2-3/4 cup sunflower seeds
1 cup brown rice flakes	1/2-1 cup chopped dates
3 tsp baking powder	1 1/2 cup soy milk
3/4 tsp salt (optional)	3 tbsp oil
	1 tbsp honey

Mix all dry ingredients in a large bowl. Form a well in the center and add the liquid ingredients. Stir just until mixed. Pour the batter in oiled or non-stick muffin tins, filling to nearly the top of the pan as these muffins do not rise very much. Bake at 400F for 20 mins. Makes 10-12.

Variation: Substitute 1 tin drained canned peaches/pears (diced) for the dates.

Currant Muffins

1/2 cup rice flour	2/3 cup water/juice
1/4 cup buckwheat/millet flour or rice polish	1/3 cup soy milk/ProSobee powder
1/4 cup washed currants	1 1/2 tbsp oil
2 egg yolks	1/4 tsp salt
	1 1/4 tsp baking powder

Preheat the oven to 400F. Put the dry ingredients in a bowl and make a well in the middle; add the liquid ingredients and the fruit. Mix. Fill oiled muffin tins 3/4 full. Bake for 15 mins.

Variation: Substitute cubed canned peaches/pears (no juice) for the currants.

Blueberry Muffins

1 tsp vanilla	6 tsp baking powder
6-8 tbsp sugar	2 cups frozen blueberries
2 cups unsifted rice flour	1 tsp salt
2 egg yolks	8 tbsp milk-free margarine
	1 1/2 cups water

Sift rice flour, baking powder, and salt together 2-3 times. Set aside. Beat margarine and sugar together. Mix well, until creamy. Gradually add egg yolks. Beat well, until light and fluffy. Add dry ingredients alternately with water and blueberries to the sugar mixture until well mixed. Fill oiled muffin cups with batter. Bake in 325F oven for 30 mins, until light brown.

6.9.5 Cookies

P4 Shortbread
Follow the recipe on p. 116 and try these variations:

Variations: Add 4 1/2 tsp currants to the dough...after dividing the dough into 3 balls, add 4 tbsp sunflower seeds to one, 1 1/2 tsp currants to another, and leave the third ball plain.

No-Bake PBJ Cookies
250 g mini marshmallows
3/4 cup safe peanut butter
1/4 cup milk-free margarine
1 tsp vanilla
6 cups Rice Flakes

1/2 cup safe jam

In a large saucepan, stir the marshmallows, peanut butter, and margarine until melted and well-blended. Remove from the heat and add the vanilla; blend in well. Stir in the cereal; blend well and cool slightly. Form the mixture into firm balls (about 2 tbsp per ball). Make an indentation in each ball with your thumb. Fill the dent with the jam. Refrigerate. Makes 2 dozen.

Sugary Cookies

2 cups milk-free margarine	2 cups sugar
1/2 tsp vanilla	2 1/2 cups rice flour
	2 egg yolks

Preheat the oven to 400F. Cream the margarine. Gradually add in the sugar. Add the egg yolks and vanilla, beating well. Gradually add the flour. Shape the dough into small balls. Put these onto ungreased cookie sheets. Bake 8-10 mins.

Rice Cereal Cookies

1/2 cup milk-free margarine	1 egg yolk + 2 tbsp water
1/2 tsp baking soda	1/2 tsp salt
1/2 cup sugar (or less)	1 tbsp water
1/2 tsp baking powder	1 cup Rice Flakes
	7/8 cup rice flour

Preheat the oven to 375F. Cream the margarine and sugar well. Beat the egg and milk together, then add this to the margarine, beating until smooth. Sift the flour, baking soda, baking powder, and salt together and add to the margarine mixture. Add the Rice Flakes and mix. Drop the cookies 2" apart on a well-oiled cookie sheet and bake 10-12 mins.

Cornstarch Shortbread

1/2 cup cornstarch	1/2 cup icing sugar
1 cup rice flour	1/4 cup milk-free margarine

Sift the dry ingredients together. Cream the margarine and add it to the dry ingredients; use your hands to mix this into a soft smooth dough. Refrigerate one hour. Preheat the oven to 300F. Shape the dough into small balls. Put the balls about 1 1/2" apart on an ungreased cookie sheet and flatten them with a lightly floured fork. Bake until the edges are lightly browned (20-25 mins).

Variation: Form the balls as above. Make a thumbprint on the top of each ball and add a dab of safe jam.

Soy Cookies

1 cup soy flour	1/4 tsp salt
1/2 tsp vanilla	3-5 tbsp apple juice
2 tsp baking powder	1/3 cup sugar
	ProSobee liquid

Preheat the oven to 350F. Combine the oil and sugar. Add vanilla. Sift the flour once before measuring and twice more after adding the baking powder and salt. Add the dry ingredients to the oil mixture along with enough juice and ProSobee to achieve desired consistency. Drop by teaspoonful onto a well-oiled cookie sheet. Bake 15 mins.

6.9.6 Pies and Crackers

P4 Soy Milk Pie Crust
Follow the recipe on p. 118 and substitute soy and/or arrowroot flour for some or all of the rice flour.

Buckwheat Pie Crust

2 cups buckwheat flour	1 tsp baking powder/soda
1 tsp salt	1/3 cup oil
	about 1/3 cup cold water

Combine the dry ingredients well. Add the oil, mixing until crumbly. Gradually add enough water to form 2 balls. Refrigerate 1 hour. Roll out each ball and place it into a pie pan, or place the ball in the pan and press it into place. Prick the dough repeatedly with a fork. Bake at 350F about 15 mins. Cool and add pie filling.

Variation: Substitute arrowroot flour for buckwheat flour.

Crackers: To make crackers, place each ball on a lightly oiled cookie sheet. Roll it out to 1/4" thick. Cut it into squares. Prick the dough repeatedly with a fork. Bake at 350F for 10 mins, or until brown (watch carefully).

6.9.7 Pie Fillings

Mushroom Filling
1 1/2 tbsp milk-free margarine
1/2 tsp safe herb
1/4 lb mushrooms, chopped

1/8 cup tofu
2 tbsp rice flour
1 tsp salt
Soy Milk Pastry (see p. 118)

Place margarine and mushrooms into a small pot. Cook until tender. Add flour, salt, and herbs; stir. Add tofu, stirring until thickened. Cool, then spoon into 4-6 precooked tart shells (you may wish to make pastry lids as well).

Seafood Filling
4 oz broken shrimp
1 tsp vinegar
4 oz soft tofu
1 tsp finely chopped parsley, fresh/dried
1 tbsp sunflower seeds, finely chopped   1/2 tsp onion juice
Soy Milk Pastry (see p. 118)

Stir together in a pot and cook till bubbling for a few minutes. Cool and spoon into 4-5 precooked tart shells, with or without lids.

6.10 Treats, Desserts, More Party Ideas

Grilling
In Phase 4, garlic powder or crushed garlic may be added to marinades, rubs, and sauces. Barbecue salmon or trout as you did whitefish in previous phases.

Sate Chicken Marinade
3 tbsp soy sauce   2 tbsp oil
3 tbsp lemon juice   pepper, salt to taste

Mix all the ingredients and marinade 1/2 Kg chicken cubes for 1 hour in the refrigerator before skewering and grilling.

P4 Grilled Fruit
Pineapple chunks, nectarine cubes or slices, and halved apricots grill well (see p. 109). Mangoes and papaya are sometimes too soft to handle, so use them carefully.

P4 Shish Kebabs
Follow the Phase 3 recipe and add:
- pineapple chunks
- cherry tomatoes
- small whole mushrooms
- prawns, precooked

Salad Rolls
Follow the Salad Roll recipes on p. 74, substituting bean sprouts for the vermicelli; shrimp, crab, or lobster for the poultry.

Potato Filling for Lettuce Wraps

5 medium potatoes	2 cloves garlic, crushed
1 medium carrot, grated	1 tbsp sunflower seeds
2 1/2 cups shredded cabbage	2 tbsp chopped parsley
2 medium onions, chopped	8 iceberg lettuce leaves

Boil the potatoes until tender, then drain and mash in a large bowl. Steam the carrots and cabbage until tender, drain, and add to the potatoes. Saute the onion and garlic; add these to the potatoes along with the hulled, chopped sunflower seeds and parsley. Mix well. Prepare the lettuce as described on p. 75 and fill with the potato mixture.

P4 Peanut Butter Spread: Stir chopped raisins or prunes, or diced pineapple and shredded coconut into peanut butter (see recipe p. 120).

Soy Butter: Mix soy flour, honey, oil, and salt to desired consistency.

Chickpea-Tahini Spread

1 large onion, minced	3 tbsp lemon juice
1 tbsp tamari sauce	plus water to make 1/2 cup
1-2 cloves minced garlic	2 cups cooked chickpeas
1/4 cup tahini	1/2 cup toasted sesame seeds
	salt to taste

Use a non-stick skillet (or use a small amount of oil if needed) to saute the onion and garlic (to taste) until translucent. If using canned chickpeas, drain and rinse them. Puree the cooked chickpeas with the sauted onion and garlic, the soy sauce, salt, tahini, and sesame seeds. Serve on rice cakes. This spread can be made hours in advance of serving.

Variation: Flavor the spread with minced fresh parsley instead of onion and garlic.

Microwave Raspberry Jam

2 cups fresh raspberries	1 envelope unflavored gelatin
1/2 cup water	3 tbsp sugar

In a microwavable bowl, stir the gelatin into the water. Let the mixture stand until the gelatin is soft (2-3 mins). Microwave the mixture to a boil on high (1-2 mins) then let stand. Puree the berries and add the sugar. Stir the berry puree into the gelatin mixture and microwave on high for 4-5 mins, then stir for 2 mins. Pour the jam into containers and refrigerate.

Variations: Replace some or all of the raspberries with strawberries, blueberries, and/or blackberries.

Crunchy Garlic

1/2 tbsp oil	1/2 cup sesame seeds
1 clove garlic, minced	1 tbsp basil

Preheat the oven to 350F. Spread the oil in a flat pan and add the other ingredients, mixing well. Spread the mixture thinly and bake 10-15 mins, stirring often. Cool, then store in the refrigerator in a glass jar with a tightly fitting lid.

Baked Pizza Crust

Crust

1 cup cornstarch	1/4 tsp salt
1/2 cup rice flour	1/2 cup water
1 tsp baking powder	1/4 cup safe oil

Topping

1/4 cup tomato paste	1/4 cup sliced mushrooms
1/4 cup chopped onion	1/2 tsp oregano
	1/2 tsp basil

Mix the crust ingredients together and press into an oiled pan. Mix the tomato paste with the seasonings. Saute the onion and mushrooms in a non-stick pan until tender. Spread the tomato paste on the crust and top with the onion and mushrooms. Bake at 425F for about 15 mins.

Pancake Bread Pizza

1 pancake bread (p. 154)	1/4 cup chopped onion
1/4 cup diced tomatoes	1/4 cup sliced mushrooms
	1 tbsp chopped fresh parsley

Saute the onions and mushrooms until tender. Remove from heat. Toast the pancake bread on a cookie sheet in a 400F oven for 5 mins. Spread the tomatoes over the bread, then scatter onions and mushrooms over top. Bake for another 5-10 mins, until the edges of the bread begins to turn brown. Serve sprinkled with parsley.

Fried Food Batter
Use a mixture of rice flour and cornstarch. For each pound of meat/vegetables, use 1/2 cup rice flour to 1/3 cup cornstarch, plus 3/4 cup water and 1 tbsp oil. Mix the flour and cornstarch, then gradually stir in the water, making a smooth mixture. Add the oil. Let the mixture stand about 30 mins at room temperature before using, to thicken it.

Millet Coating
Use millet meal or crushed puffed millet (freeze first to make crushing easier), seasoned with safe herbs and salt if desired, to coat chicken/turkey pieces.

6.10.1 Gravies and Sauces

Non-wheat Gravy
Use a wheat flour substitute instead of your usual thickener to make gravy from drippings.

P4 Peanut Butter Sauce
Follow the P3 recipe (see p. 110) and add 1 tsp garlic powder and/or add 2 tbsp coconut milk to thicken the sauce.

Lemon/Lime Spark
See p. 140, using this over steamed fish or barbecued chicken.

Tahini Sauce
3 tbsp tahini
1/4 cup lemon juice

1 tbsp water
1 tbsp chopped parsley
2 tbsp safe oil

Combine all the ingredients, mixing well.

6.10.2 Snacks and Dessert

P4 Granola
Follow the Phase 3 recipe on p. 122 and add puffed millet along with/instead of puffed rice. Add chopped prunes or raisins with the sesame seeds.

Phase 4

Trail Mix
Combine chopped prunes or raisins, hulled sunflower or pumpkin seeds, and puffed rice or puffed millet cereal.

Fruit Leather
1 or more large can pears, unsweetened
1 or more large can peaches, unsweetened

Drain the pears and peaches well. Puree the fruit in a blender. Cover a cookie sheet with plastic wrap. Spread the fruit puree evenly over the cookie sheet. Dry in an oven set at the lowest temperature, with the door partially open (make sure small children and pets do not have access to the oven). Check every 4-8 hours. It may take 20 or more hours to dry the fruit, depending on the thickness of the leather and how much liquid is in it.

Rice Cereal Squares
1/2 tsp vanilla
3 cups Rice Krispies
2 tbsp milk-free margarine
125 g marshmallows

Melt the marshmallows and margarine. Add the cereal, coating it thoroughly with the marshmallow mixture. Press into a greased/oiled pan and refrigerate. When set, cut into squares.

P4 Fruit Salad
Choose any combination, including those fruits mentioned on p. 3.6.3 and 4.10.2 if desired, toss together, and chill: diced pineapple, apricots, cranberries,
currants, nectarines, cherries, blackberries, mangoes, papaya, oranges, and coconut.

Sweet and Sour Fruit

75g brown sugar	1/2 tbsp lemon juice
1 tbsp warm water	1/2 small cucumber
1/2 tbsp soy sauce	1 mango
1 Granny Smith apple	1 orange

Mix the sugar with the water until a paste forms. Stir in the soy sauce, mixing well. Peel and core the apple. Cut it in thin slices and sprinkle with lemon juice. Peel the cucumber and cut it in half. Remove the seeds and cut the cucumber in thick strips. Peel the mango and remove the pit, cutting the fruit in chunks. Peel the orange and remove the white strings. Separate the orange segments and cut each in chunks. In a bowl, mix the apple, cucumber, mango, and orange. Refrigerate until serving time. Then stir the sugar sauce (if the sauce is hardened, add a bit more water) and divide it among 4 bowls. Put a quarter of the fruit mixture in each bowl and serve.

Cubed Cantaloupe Salad
1 large cantaloupe
2 tbsp lemon juice

1 tbsp minced mint
2 tbsp lime juice
1 tbsp honey

Cut the cantelope,remove seeds and cut into cubes. Put the cubed cantaloupe into a bowl. Mix the lemon and lime juices, honey, and chopped mint, pouring this over the melon. Toss gently, cover, and refrigerate for 1 hour or more before serving. Variation: Any melon, except watermelon, may be substituted for the cantaloupe.

Apple Tapioca
3/4 cup tapioca
7 baking apples

2 1/2 cup boiling water
1/2 cup sugar
1/2 tsp salt

Put the tapioca in the top saucepan of a double boiler, cover with cold water, and soak for 1 hour. Drain, then add the boiling water and salt to the tapioca and add water to the bottom of the double boiler. Cook until the tapioca is translucent. Halve, core, and peel the apples. Arrange the apple halves, round end down, in an oiled baking dish. Fill the apples with the sugar and cover with the tapioca. Bake at 400F until the apples (about 30 mins).

P4 Rice Pudding
Follow the Phase 1 recipe on p. 3.6.3, using pineapple or apricots instead of canned peaches.

Blueberry Tapioca
2 1/2 cups blueberries, fresh or
frozen (thawed)

1/2 cup water
1/2 cup sugar
2 tbsp tapioca

Mix all ingredients in a 2 qt saucepan. Let stand for 5 mins, then bring to a boil, stirring constantly. Serve warm or chilled.

Peach Tapioca
2 peach halves, sliced
2 tsp sugar

1 tbsp tapioca
1/2 cup peach juice + water

Drain the peaches. Mix the juice with enough water to make 1/2 cup and add the tapioca, cooking it until it is translucent. Add 1 tsp sugar and salt to the tapioca. Line a baking dish with the peaches and sprinkle them with 1 tsp sugar. Cover with tapioca and bake for 20 mins in a moderate oven.

Fruit Juice Tapioca
4 cups safe fruit juice (part water if desired)
1/2 cup tapioca

Soak the tapioca in the juice for 10 mins. Sweeten with sugar/honey to taste. Heat the tapioca to boiling, then chill and serve with fruit.

Fruit Tapioca
2 tbsp quick cooking tapioca	dash of salt
1 large can peach slices	cherries, halved and pitted
2 tbsp sugar	1/2 cup water

Mix the tapioca, sugar, salt, and water in a 2 qt microwavable bowl. Microwave on high until the tapioca is thickened (2-4 mins). Drain the peaches, reserving the juice. Chop each peach slice into thirds and add these and the juice to the tapioca, then chill several hours. Stir in the cherries just before serving. Variation: Try any fruit combination of your choice.

Cornstarch Pudding
1 1/2 cups safe fruit puree	1 1/2 cups water
2 tsp sugar	5 tsp cornstarch

Combine the fruit, sugar, and water in the top of a double boiler. Slowly add the cornstarch, stirring well so the pudding remains smooth. Simmer for 1/2 hour.

P4 Fruit Sherbets
Follow the recipes on p. 44 and 84 with the following variations.

Peach Sherbet: Add 2 tbsp minced mint after initial pureeing.

Strawberry Sherbet: Add 1/4 cup lemon juice with the sugar.

Mango Sherbet: Pit and puree 5 mangos. In a large bowl, combine the mangos, 1 cup Sherbet Syrup, and 2 tbsp lime juice. Freeze as instructed in Phase 1.

Pineapple Sherbet: Cube and puree 2 cups ripe pineapple or 2 cups unsweetened canned pineapple with juice. Freeze as instructed in Phase 1.

Gelatin Popsicles
Dissolve one package unflavored gelatin in a cup of boiling water. Stir in 1 1/2 cups of safe fruit juice and sweeten to taste with sugar or honey. Pour into popsicle molds or ice cube trays and freeze.

Soy-Gelatin Ice Cream
1 envelope unflavored gelatin
2 cups fresh or thawed strawberries

1 1/2 cups cold water
1 cup Prosobee Ready-to-Use
2/3 cup sugar

Dissolve the gelatin in 1/2 cup water over low heat then cool. Add the remaining ingredients. Freeze as directed for P1 Sherbets (see p. 44).

Variations: Substitute other safe berries for some or all of the strawberries...add vanilla after adding the berries.

Toppings

Cranberry Sauce
Combine 2 cups water and 2 cups sugar in a large pot. Bring to a boil and boil 5 mins. Add 4 cups cranberries and bring to a boil, boiling for 5 more mins. Cool, then cover and refrigerate overnight before using.

6.10.3 Beverages

Fruit Blend
1 cup fresh orange juice
1/4 cantaloupe, cubed

1/4 lemon, cubed
1 cup ice

Blend all ingredients until frothy. Serves 2.

Cranberry Cocktail
1/3 cup cranberry juice
1/4 cup pear nectar

1/4 cup orange juice
ice (if desired)

Blend all ingredients and serve.
To improve the flavor of soy milk, blend 1 tbsp honey (with or without the suggestions on p. 125) into 1 cup of soy milk.

P4 Fruit Soy Drink
Follow the Phase 3 recipe on p. 5.9.3, substituting 1/2 cup of apricot nectar for the peach/pear nectar.

Pineapple Soy Drink
1/2 cup soy milk

1 tsp sugar
1/2 cup pineapple juice

Blend the ingredients well and serve immediately.

Mango Soy Drink
1 medium mango, peeled and chopped
1 cup soy milk
1 tbsp honey

Blend all the ingredients until smooth. Serve chilled.

Index

Appendix

DAILY PORTIONS OF CORE DIET FOODS:

2-3   *Rice, Grains, and Flours portions*

4-6   *Cooked Vegetable portions*

3-4   *Raw Vegetable portions*

2   *Fruit portions*

1-2   *High Protein portions*

1-3tsp   *Vegetable oil*

Water 1 to 2 litre(s) at least

Portion size is approximately one cup of cooked or cut vegetables, or fruit; one cup of cooked rice or caloric equivalent in rice products. The following tables of nutritional values for food specify portion size.

CORE DIET MEAL PLANS:

Each well-balanced meal contains a mix of foods in the following order. Vegetables have been grouped according to culinary, nutritional and botanical characteristics. Consult the following list for vegetable and fruit groupings.

1   Rice, Grains, and Flours portion

3-4   Cooked Vegetable portions

         - 1 Group A
         - 1 Group B
         - 1 Group C
         - 1 Group D
         - 1 Group F (optional)
         - 1 Group G (optional)
         - 1 Group H (optional)

1-2   Raw Vegetable portions
         - 2 Group E

1   High Protein portion

1   Fruit portion

Core Program Food List

Vegetables by Group

A: Yellow/Orange Vegetables

carrots (Umbelliferae)
yams (Dioscoreaceae)
sweet potatoes (Convolvulaceae)
squash (Curcurbita)
pumpkin (Curcurbita)
parsnips (Umbelliferae)
turnips (Cruciferae)

B: Legumes

green beans
peas
wax beans
lentils
lima beans
white beans
split peas
chickpeas (garbanzos)
tofu

C: Brassica (Cruciferae)

broccoli
cauliflower
brussels sprouts
cabbage
kale
kohlrabi

D: Leaf Vegetables

lettuce (Compositae)
celery (Umbelliferae)
spinach (Chenopodiaceae)
bok choy (Cruciferae)
beet greens (Chenopodiaceae
chard (Chenopodiaceae

E: Salad Vegetables

zucchini (Curcurbita)
cucumbers (Curcurbita)
onions (Allium)
mushrooms
chives (Allium)
carrots (Umbelliferae)
peas (Leguminosae)
broccoli (Cruciferae)
cauliflower (Cruciferae)
cabbage (Cruciferae)
lettuce (Compositae)
celery (Umbelliferae)
spinach (Chenopodiaceae)
chard (Chenopodiaceae)
turnips (Cruciferae)
radishes (Cruciferae)
beets (Chenopodiaceae)
bean sprouts (Leguminosae)

F: Optional Vegetables

zucchini, cooked (Curcurbita)
asparagus (Liliaceae)
beets (Chenopodiaceae)
bean sprouts (Leguminosae)

G: Flavoring Vegetables

onions (Allium)
mushrooms
chives (Allium)
leeks (Allium)

H: Nightshade Vegetables

potatoes (Solanaceae)
tomatoes (Solanaceae)
green peppers

Rice, Grains, and Flours

white rice (Gramineae)
rice cakes
rice crackers
rice cereal
rice flour
rice starch
rice noodles
rice paper
brown rice (Gramineae)
Basmati rice (Gramineae)
buckwheat (Polygonaceae)
millet (Gramineae)
tapioca (Euphorbiaceae)
cornstarch (Gramineae)
arrowroot flour (Maranta)
soy flour (Leguminosae)

Fruits

pears
peaches
applesauce
blueberries
watermelon
cantaloupe
honeydew melon
avocado
raspberries
strawberries
plums
grapes
pineapple
apples
apricots
cranberries
currants
nectarines
cherries
mangoes
papaya
blackberries
oranges

High Protein

chicken
turkey
whitefish
beef
lamb
tuna
salmon
tofu
shellfish
crustaceans

Dairy Substitutes

infant soy formulas
soy milk
tofu products
milk-free margarine
soy-lecithin spread
clarified butter (ghee)
Rice Dream

Flavorings

salt
sugar
oregano
thyme
rosemary
parsley
basil
garlic
pepper
dill
bay leaves
celery seed
marjoram
mustard
sunflower seeds
pumpkin seeds
sesame seeds
soy sauce
teriyaki sauce
vinegar
lemon juice
lime juice
honey
vanilla
carob powder

Baking

baking soda
baking powder
egg yolk (avoid egg white)
egg substitutes yeast

Vegetable Oil

safflower oil
sunflower oil
olive oil

NUTRIENT ANALYSIS OF CORE DIET FOODS

Nutritive Components for Core Diet Foods

Food Name	KCAL Kc	PROT Gm	CARB Gm	FAT Gm	FIBC Gm	CALC Mg	MAG Mg	IRON Mg	V-C Mg	THIA Mg	NIAC Mg	V-B6 Mg
RICE-WHITE-PARBOIL-COOKED	185	4.0	41.0	0.0	0.18	33	-	1.40	0	0.190	2.1	0.74
RICE-WHITE-LONG GRAIN-COOK	225	4.0	50.0	0.0	0.21	21	16	1.80	0	0.230	2.1	0.87
RICE-BROWN-LONG-COOKED-HOT	232	4.9	49.7	1.2	-	23	-	1.00	0	0.180	2.7	-
RICE CAKE-REGULAR	35	0.7	7.6	0.3	-	-	-	-	-	-	-	-
CHICK-BREAST-NO SKIN-ROAST	284	53.4	0.0	6.1	0.00	26	50	1.78	0	0.120	23.6	1.02
TURKEY-LIGHT-NO SKIN-ROAST	269	51.5	0.0	5.5	0.00	33	48	2.31	0	0.104	11.8	0.92
CARROTS-BOIL-DRAIN-SLICED	70	1.7	16.3	0.3	2.30	48	20	0.96	4	0.054	0.8	0.38
CARROT-RAW-WHOLE-SCRAPED	67	1.6	15.8	0.3	1.63	41	24	0.78	15	0.152	1.4	0.23
PEARS-CAN/JUICE	123	0.9	32.1	0.2	1.22	21	17	0.71	4	0.027	0.5	-
PEACHES-CAN/WATER PACK	58	1.1	14.9	0.1	0.75	6	12	0.77	7	0.020	1.3	0.05
BEANS-SNAP-GREEN-RAW-BOIL	44	2.4	9.9	0.4	1.79	58	32	1.60	12	0.093	0.8	0.07
BROCCOLI-RAW-BOIL-DRAIN	46	4.6	8.7	0.4	1.88	178	94	1.78	98	0.128	1.2	0.31
BROCCOLI-RAW	24	2.6	4.6	0.3	0.98	42	22	0.78	82	0.058	0.6	0.14
PEAS-GREEN-FROZ-BOIL-DRAIN	126	8.2	22.8	0.4	3.42	38	46	2.52	16	0.452	2.4	0.18
PEAS-EDIBLE PODDED-RAW	61	4.1	11.0	0.3	3.63	62	35	3.01	87	0.218	0.9	0.23
YAMS-BOIL OR BAKE-DRAIN	158	2.0	37.5	0.2	-	19	25	0.70	17	0.129	0.8	0.31
SQUASH-WINTER-BAKE-MASH	79	1.8	17.9	1.3	1.46	28	16	0.67	20	0.174	1.4	0.15
SQUASH-ZUCCHINI-RAW-BOIL	28	1.1	7.1	0.1	0.90	24	38	0.64	8	0.074	0.8	0.14
SQUASH-ZUCCHINI-RAW-SLICED	19	1.5	3.8	0.2	0.58	20	28	0.55	12	0.091	0.5	0.12
CAULIFLOWER-RAW-BOIL-DRAIN	30	2.3	5.7	0.2	1.02	34	14	0.52	69	0.078	0.7	0.25
CAULIFLOWER-RAW-CHOPPED	24	2.0	4.9	0.2	0.85	29	14	0.58	72	0.076	0.6	0.23
APPLESAUCE-CAN-UNSWEETENED	106	0.4	27.6	0.1	1.30	7	7	0.29	3	0.032	0.5	0.06

NUTRIENT ANALYSIS OF CORE DIET FOODS

Nutritive Components for Core Diet Foods

Food Name	KCAL Kc	PROT Gm	CARB Gm	FAT Gm	FIBC Gm	CALC Mg	MAG Mg	IRON Mg	V-C Mg	THIA Mg	NIAC Mg	V-B6 Mg
FISH-SOLE/FLOUNDER-BAKED	99	20.5	0.0	1.3	0.00	15	50	0.29	-	0.068	1.9	0.20
FISH-HALIBUT-BROILED-DRY	119	22.7	0.0	2.5	0.00	51	91	0.91	-	0.059	6.1	0.34
LETTUCE-ICEBERG-RAW-CHOP	7	0.6	1.1	0.1	0.33	10	5	0.27	2	0.025	0.1	0.02
CUCUMBER-RAW-SLICED	14	0.6	3.0	0.1	0.62	14	12	0.28	5	0.032	0.3	0.05
BLUEBERRIES-RAW	82	1.0	20.5	0.6	1.88	9	7	0.24	19	0.070	0.5	0.05
MELONS-HONEYDEW-RAW	60	0.8	15.6	0.2	1.02	10	12	0.12	42	0.131	1.0	0.10
MELONS-CANTALOUPE-RAW	57	1.4	13.4	0.4	0.58	17	17	0.34	68	0.058	0.9	0.18
WATERMELON-RAW	50	1.0	11.5	0.7	0.48	13	17	0.28	15	0.128	0.3	0.23
AVOCADO-RAW-CALIFORNIA	306	3.6	12.0	30.0	3.65	19	70	2.04	14	0.187	3.3	0.48
BRUSSEL SPROUTS-RAW-BOIL	60	4.0	13.5	0.8	2.14	56	32	1.88	97	0.166	0.9	0.28
FLOUR-RICE	479	7.5	107.0	0.4	-	11	35	3.60	0	0.520	7.2	-
PEACHES-RAW-WHOLE	37	0.6	9.6	0.1	0.56	5	6	0.10	6	0.015	0.9	0.02
APPLES-RAW-UNPEELED	81	0.3	21.1	0.5	1.06	10	6	0.25	8	0.023	0.1	0.07
APPLE-RAW-PEELED	72	0.2	19.0	0.4	0.69	5	4	0.09	5	0.022	0.1	0.06
PEARS-RAW-BARTLET-UNPEELED	98	0.6	25.1	0.7	2.32	19	9	0.41	7	0.033	0.2	0.03
ASPARAGUS-FROZ-BOIL-SPEARS	50	5.3	8.8	0.8	1.51	41	23	1.15	44	0.117	1.9	0.04
CABBAGE-WHITE MUSTARD-BOIL	20	2.6	3.0	0.3	1.02	158	18	1.77	44	0.054	0.7	-
CABBAGE-WHITE MUSTARD-RAW	9	1.0	1.5	0.1	0.42	74	13	0.56	32	0.028	0.4	-
CABBAGE-COMMON-BOIL-DRAIN	31	1.4	6.9	0.4	0.87	48	22	0.57	35	0.083	0.3	0.09
CABBAGE-COMMON-RAW-SHRED	22	1.1	4.8	0.2	0.72	42	14	0.50	43	0.045	0.3	0.09
HAMBURGER-GROUND-REG-BAKED	244	19.6	0.0	17.8	0.00	8	13	2.05	0	0.026	4.0	0.20
RASPBERRIES-RAW	61	1.1	14.2	0.7	3.69	27	22	0.70	31	0.037	1.1	0.07

NUTRIENT ANALYSIS OF CORE DIET FOODS

Nutritive Components for Core Diet Foods

Food Name	KCAL Kc	PROT Gm	CARB Gm	FAT Gm	FIBC Gm	CALC Mg	MAG Mg	IRON Mg	V-C Mg	THIA Mg	NIAC Mg	V-B6 Mg
STRAWBERRIES-RAW-WHOLE	45	0.9	10.5	0.6	0.79	21	16	0.57	85	0.030	0.3	0.09
MUSHROOMS-BOIL-DRAIN	18	1.5	3.6	0.4	0.58	6	6	1.23	3	0.053	3.1	0.06
MUSHROOMS-RAW-CHOPPED	18	1.5	3.3	0.3	0.52	4	8	0.86	2	0.072	2.9	0.07
CHIVES-RAW-CHOPPED	1	0.1	0.1	0.0	0.03	2	2	0.05	2	0.003	0.0	0.01
PLUMS-RAW-PRUNE TYPE	20	0.0	6.0	0.0	0.17	2	2	0.10	1	0.010	0.1	0.02
GRAPES-RAW-AMERICAN TYPE	58	0.6	15.8	0.3	0.70	3	5	0.27	4	0.085	0.3	0.10
LAMB-CHOP/RIB-LEAN-BROILED	120	16.0	0.0	6.0	0.00	6	13	1.10	-	0.090	3.4	0.16
SPINACH-RAW-BOIL-DRAIN	41	5.3	6.8	0.5	1.59	244	157	6.42	18	0.171	0.9	0.44
SPINACH-RAW-CHOPPED	12	1.6	2.0	0.2	0.50	56	44	1.52	16	0.044	0.4	0.11
PINEAPPLE-CAN/JUICE	150	1.0	39.2	0.2	0.87	34	35	0.70	24	0.238	0.7	-
FISH-TUNA-WHITE-CAN/WATER	116	22.7	0.0	2.1	0.00	-	-	0.51	-	0.003	4.9	-
ONIONS-MATURE-BOIL-DRAIN	58	1.9	13.2	0.3	0.88	58	22	0.42	12	0.088	0.2	0.38
ONIONS-MATURE-RAW-CHOPPED	54	1.9	11.7	0.4	0.70	40	16	0.58	13	0.096	0.2	0.25
GARLIC-RAW-CLOVE	4	0.2	1.0	0.0	0.05	5	1	0.05	1	0.006	0.0	-
SEEDS-SUNFLOWER-DRIED	821	32.8	27.0	71.4	5.99	168	509	9.75	-	3.290	6.5	1.81
SEEDS-PUMPKIN/SQUASH-DRIED	747	33.9	24.6	63.3	3.07	59	738	20.70	-	0.290	2.4	0.12

SAMPLE NUTRIENT ANALYSIS OF RECIPES

STIR-FRIED MIXED VEGETABLES

Food Name	KCAL Kc	PROT Gm	CARB Gm	FAT Gm	FIBC Gm	CALC Mg	MAG Mg	IRON Mg
VEGETABLE OIL-SAFFLOWER	40.1	0.000	0.00	4.542	0.000	0.0	0.0	0.000
SQUASH-ZUCCHINI-RAW-BOIL	42.0	1.710	10.62	0.150	1.350	36.0	57.0	0.960
CARROTS-BOIL-DRAIN-SLICED	52.5	1.275	12.23	0.210	1.725	36.0	15.0	0.720
PARSLEY-RAW-CHOPPED	0.6	0.044	0.14	0.006	0.024	2.6	0.8	0.124
BROCCOLI-RAW-BOIL-DRAIN	23.0	2.320	4.34	0.220	0.940	89.0	47.0	0.890
ASPARAGUS-RAW-BOIL-SPEARS	11.0	1.165	1.98	0.140	0.375	11.0	8.5	0.295
	-----	-----	-----	-----	-----	-----	-----	-----
Total for Recipe:	169.2	6.514	29.30	5.268	4.414	174.6	128.3	2.989

Nutritive Components for Chicken Soup (one dish meal)

Food Name	KCAL Kc	PROT Gm	CARB Gm	FAT Gm	FIBC Gm	CALC Mg	MAG Mg	IRON Mg
CARROTS-BOIL-DRAIN-SLICED	35.00	0.850	8.150	0.140	1.150	24.00	10.00	0.480
CHICKEN BREAST-NO SKIN-ROAST	284.0	53.40	0.000	6.140	0.000	26.00	50.00	1.780
BROCCOLI-RAW-BOIL-DRAIN	23.00	2.320	4.340	0.220	0.940	89.00	47.00	0.890
SQUASH-SUMMER-BOIL-SLICED	18.00	0.815	3.880	0.280	0.540	24.00	22.00	0.320
RICE-WHITE-INSTANT-HOT	90.00	2.000	20.00	0.000	0.083	2.500	6.600	0.650
VEGETABLE OIL-SAFFLOWER	10.04	0.000	0.000	1.135	0.000	0.000	0.000	0.000
	-----	-----	-----	-----	-----	-----	-----	-----
Total for Recipe	460.0	59.38	36.37	7.915	2.712	165.5	135.6	4.120

Nutritive Components for a Single Serving of
TURKEY VEGETABLE SOUP

Food Name	KCAL Kc	PROT Gm	CARB Gm	FAT Gm	FIBC Gm	CALC Mg	MAG Mg	IRON Mg
TURK-BREAST-NO SKIN-ROAST	274.6	61.18	0.00	1.496	0.000	25.27	59.18	3.112
CARROTS-BOIL-DRAIN-SLICED	39.4	0.96	9.17	0.157	1.294	27.00	11.25	0.540
CELERY-PASCAL-RAW-STALK	3.0	0.13	0.72	0.025	0.140	7.00	2.50	0.095
SALT-TABLE SALT	0.0	0.00	0.00	0.000	0.000	7.00	0.00	0.000
PEPPER-BLACK	0.3	0.01	0.09	0.004	0.018	0.56	0.25	0.038
BASIL-GROUND	0.5	0.03	0.11	0.008	0.031	3.75	0.75	0.074
WATER	0.0	0.00	0.00	0.000	0.000	12.50	5.00	0.025
MUSHROOMS-RAW-CHOPPED	4.5	0.36	0.82	0.075	0.130	1.00	2.00	0.215
FLOUR-RICE	29.9	0.47	6.69	0.025	-	0.69	2.19	0.225
Total for Recipe:	352.3	63.14	17.59	1.791	1.612	84.77	83.12	4.324

STUFFED ZUCCHINI #2

Food Name	KCAL Kc	PROT Gm	CARB Gm	FAT Gm	FIBC Gm	CALC Mg	MAG Mg	IRON Mg
SQUASH-ZUCCHINI-RAW-BOIL	42.0	1.710	10.62	0.150	1.350	36.00	57.00	0.960
RICE-WHITE-PARBOIL-COOKED	92.5	2.000	20.50	0.000	0.088	16.50	-	0.700
MUSHROOMS-RAW-CHOPPED	4.5	0.365	0.82	0.075	0.130	1.00	2.00	0.215
CELERY-PASCAL-RAW-DICED	4.5	0.200	1.09	0.035	0.205	11.00	3.50	0.145
THYME-GROUND	2.0	0.065	0.45	0.050	0.130	13.00	1.50	0.865
SALT-TABLE SALT	0.0	0.000	0.00	0.000	0.000	0.88	0.00	0.000
Total for Recipe:	145.5	4.340	33.47	0.310	1.903	78.38	64.00	2.885